BOUNTIFUL
BONSAI

Create Instant Indoor Container Gardens with Edible Fruits, Herbs and Flowers

RICHARD W. BENDER

BOUNTIFUL BONSAI, First Edition (2014)
Create Instant Indoor Container Gardens
with Edible Fruits, Herbs and Flowers
by Richard W. Bender

Photo Credits:

John Baughman (www.jbaughmanphoto.com): front cover, front flap (top), inside front cover (bottom), 4, 9 (top), 10, 13–14, 18, 21–27, 32, 38–39, 40 (top), 41–44, 46 (bottom), 48–49, 52, 54, 56, 59, 62, 64, 66–71, 75, 80–81, 86, 91–93, 96, 105, 108–111, 126, inside back cover (bottom), back flap (top)

Richard W. Bender: front flap (bottom), inside front cover (top), 2, 8, 9 (bottom), 11, 35, 40 (bottom), 46 (top), 73, 90, 102–104, 107, 114, 119–120, 122–124, inside back cover (top), back cover

TUTTLE Publishing

Tokyo | Rutland, Vermont | Singapore

Dedication

When I was young, my mother told me,
"Boy, the way you like to eat, you better learn
how to cook." I grew up with a large vegetable
garden and operated a produce stand to earn
money until I went to college. My family also
collected wild mushrooms, fruits, and game
animals in the woods. Following Mom's advice,
I learned to look for food everywhere, and
learned to cook what I found. I even expect my
houseplants to provide a useful crop.
I dedicate this book to my mother,
Marie K. Bender.

CONTENTS

CHAPTER 1

Bonsai: An Overview

W hile the history of bonsai goes back several hundred years in its modern form as developed by the Japanese, there is no doubt that mankind has shaped plants for as long as humans have grown and tended them. The first plants grown in containers were most likely valuable herbs or food plants that the growers wanted to transport or protect from harm. The oldest images of potted plants come from Egyptian paintings; Hindu doctors were known to keep medicinal plants in pots for easy cultivation and transportation around 1000 BCE.

Bonsai became a well-developed art in China during the first millennium CE, as evidenced by the first writings and paintings about bonsai as an art form. By the time of the Sung dynasty, around 1000 CE, bonsai as an art form was spreading throughout Chinese culture with paintings, poetry, and technical instructions in the literature of the time. It was probably around this time that bonsai was introduced into Japan, most likely by Buddhist monks; the first written records of bonsai appeared there around 1300 CE.

Bonsai developed into its modern form in Japan with very strict styles and conventions that mirrored the structured society in which it developed.

Specimens were mostly grown outdoors, and were often tended for generations, passing from father to son, using native plant varieties that were suited to the local climatic conditions. Western society was exposed to the art of bonsai during the twentieth century, particularly during the aftermath of World War II. Many American GIs who spent time in Japan after the war became fascinated by aspects of Japanese culture, and bonsai was an interest that some of them brought home. The *Karate Kid* movies, the first of which came out in 1984, introduced bonsai to a new generation of children in the US. In fact, 1989's *Karate Kid, Part III* opened with the karate master Mr. Miyagi fulfilling his lifelong dream of opening a bonsai shop. A bonsai theme was prominent in that movie, including recapturing a "repatriated" bonsai tree that Mr. Miyagi had planted back in the wild after bringing it to America from Okinawa. Throughout the 1980s, as a bonsai artist managing several garden centers I witnessed an amazing number of children, primarily boys, who were looking for bonsai "like Mr. Miyagi's trees." Millions of children were exposed to and fascinated by bonsai as a result of this type of mass-media attention. Traditional Japanese bonsai had captured the imagination of the West.

Unfortunately, many of the resulting attempts at cultivation were unsuccessful. Millions of juniper bonsai died in people's homes as buyers reached out to embrace a fad without understanding the conditions required to keep these trees alive. Traditional Japanese-style bonsai primarily uses outdoor trees that require a cold dormant period to thrive—junipers, pines, and maples. These outdoor varieties are not suitable for use as houseplants, and seldom last long indoors. As the art of bonsai gained a foothold in the West, however, more indoor varieties were used, because people wanted bonsai that could be put in the house and treated like houseplants.

The art of bonsai has developed with several different philosophies or schools of thought beyond the traditional Japanese style. The use of strictly indoor varieties has become most prominent of these, embracing many new varieties beyond the usual ficus and serissa that were among the few tropical varieties used by traditional Chinese and Japanese bonsai artists. A sideline to this is the specialization in flowering varieties. Another philosophy, similar to traditional Japanese-style bonsai, strives to use only local varieties native to the region and grow them outdoors.

An older style that seems to be losing favor is the collection of wild, natural bonsai. This is understandable, as the field trips to wild areas to collect "natural" bonsai that this tradition involved resulted in the defacement of natural areas and losses from digging up trees in the wild. Modern environmental ethics preclude digging wild bonsai from our dwindling natural areas.

There is still a place, however, for collecting "wild" natural bonsai when cleaning brush from cultivated fields, lawns, or vacant lots. Some amazing bonsai can be collected when cleaning out old yards and fields, without damaging our natural areas. A friend clearing brush from a lot collected one of the most unique bonsai I've ever seen, a wild elm with a two-inch diameter trunk that was cut off twelve inches above the ground and potted into a six-inch plastic pot. A year later, this stump had developed a fine, strong set of roots and a fringe of branches growing around the rim of the stump. My friend had always wanted a hollow-trunked bonsai, so as a demonstration at a bonsai show, he used a one-inch bit and a hand drill to hollow the trunk straight down from the top to an inch above the ground and in from the side to meet the bottom of that hole. He then took a two-handed electric router and carved a jagged "lightning strike" down several inches from one side of the top and shaped the hole from the side. As wood chips were hitting the roof of the greenhouse, the traditional bonsai artists in attendance gaped in amazement at the scene unfolding in front of them. I saw that tree again a year later, and it had survived the harsh treatment.

Using herbs as subjects for bonsai was only mentioned a handful of times in the previous history of bonsai writing before the publication of my article "Herbs as Bonsai" in the November 1987 edition of *Horticulture* magazine, which was followed by my book *Herbal Bonsai* in 1996. Herbal bonsai changes the whole timescale of bonsai development because of its comparatively fast growth. Impressive specimens can be created in as little as one growing season with a plant such as rosemary, yet these plants can be kept alive in pots for fifty years or more. A moderately large herbal bonsai can provide homegrown fresh herbs in sufficient quantity to supply a household. Growing herbs indoors can be a little trickier than cultivating tropical plant varieties, but the idea of consuming your bonsai trimmings leads naturally to considering a fruiting bonsai that provides a usable harvest.

It seems a little incongruous to think of a bonsai tree providing enough harvest to amount to much, but bonsai don't have to be miniature. Even traditional Japanese classifications include bonsai up to six feet tall. An edible fig or a citrus tree of that size can provide an amazing amount of fruit. I have harvested enough of these fruits to make jam and to ferment into wine (although I will admit to freezing an entire crop and using a couple of crops to make two cases of wine). A friend asked whether I pour tiny glasses of bonsai wine. I replied, "Of course, we use sake cups to help provide the proper ceremonial courtesy when sharing such a rare vintage."

Limequat Mariachi wine.

Citrus trees have an added advantage in that most citrus fruits can sit on a tree for several months after becoming ripe without going bad, and can be picked fresh when ready to use. With a small collection of several varieties of citrus, it is possible to have fresh citrus to pick nearly 365 days a year, even in places like my home in the Colorado mountains. You may not be able to pick one every single day of the year, but it is quite reasonable to expect to pick a couple of fruits a week for cooking purposes. Varieties with smaller fruits have more appeal strictly as bonsai specimens, and also provide a bigger crop than large-fruited varieties. These small varieties include calamondin orange, kumquat, Key lime, and the harder-to-find limequat (a lime-kumquat cross). The limequat is the heaviest bearer of fruit in my experience, and my calamondins here in Colorado usually produce two crops a year.

Though many people grow ornamental ficus trees in their homes, they seldom grow the species that produce edible figs. There are many cultivated varieties, of which *Ficus carica* is the most prevalent. The "standard" ficus, which resembles a lollipop stuck in a five-gallon nursery pot, is one of the most common houseplants sold in the plant industry, and is widely used in interior landscaping. An edible fig variety of the same size can produce several dozen fresh figs every summer. There are some differences in care and appearance between ornamental and edible figs that might seem daunting, but the benefit of obtaining fresh fruit from houseplants outweighs many other considerations.

Many dedicated coffee and tea drinkers don't realize that these plants are rather easy to grow as houseplants. The camellia, a popular

Limequats, a lime-kumquat cross, are a little smaller than an egg and turn yellow when ripe. Though sour, they have great flavor, and can be used peel and all in many kinds of cooking.

This bowl of limequats made seven half-pints of limequat marmalade; the rest was fermented into three cases of wine.

flowering tree that blooms in mid-winter, is often grown as a houseplant in northern climates. *Camellia sinensis*, the tea plant, has smaller, less spectacular flowers than ornamental camellia varieties, but the white flowers are numerous and the blooming season lasts longer. Green tea plants and seeds can be found and purchased online. A regular tea drinker may not be able to grow their entire supply, but any amount of homegrown tea is a worthy addition to a collection of teas.

Coffee trees can be easy to find. Large trees produce many beans; some of the large foliage growers in Florida will throw a handful of coffee beans into four-inch pots and include the seedlings in their shipments of mixed-foliage plants. I've found these pots of coffee trees mixed into inexpensive foliage collections at garden centers all over the country. Coffee trees take some time

This thirty-inch dwarf pomegranate, cultivated from a five-gallon nursery stock plant, has been in training for seven months.

These fruits are considered ornamental. While their quality doesn't compare to that of full-sized commercial pomegranates, they are beautiful and technically edible.

to begin producing beans, but I have not only produced beans in Colorado from plants that started as six-inch seedlings, but have seen a six-foot coffee tree in Montana so loaded with beans there was fear the branches would break. Again, houseplants cannot be expected to offer a full supply of coffee, but the ability to offer coffee harvested from the beautiful tree in your living room on special occasions is priceless.

A few edible species are becoming more common in indoor tropical bonsai collections, particularly Australian cherry (*Eugenia paniculata*), dwarf pomegranate (*Punica granatum* var. *nana*), Barbados cherry (*Malpighia emarginata*), and Natal plum (*Carissa macrocarpa*). All of these are easy to find and have several varieties available, some of which are known to produce more fruit than others. Natal plums are used extensively in landscaping

Miniature Australian cherries seldom flower. This specimen is sixteen inches tall.

in the desert Southwest and should be easy to find at nurseries in that area. Dwarf pomegranates, which can flower and fruit heavily, are becoming very popular as bonsai specimens. Large fruiting pomegranate varieties have larger leaves that may go deciduous for a period; they aren't as attractive as the dwarf variety, but they do bear much larger fruit. The heavier flowering and fruiting varieties of Australian cherry are widely sold at local nurseries as large topiary specimens, but the miniature varieties that make the most spectacular bonsai only flower sporadically, and in twenty years of growing them, I have never seen them bear fruit.

Several species of guava, including the strawberry guava (*Psidium cattleanum*), lemon guava (*Psidium littorale*) and pineapple guava (*Feijoa sellowiana*), produce delightful fruit and can be grown indoors. Papayas can be grown from seed out of fruit from the market; I have grown them from seed to fruiting in Colorado. Avocados, easily sprouted from their large pits, can be shaped into interesting bonsai, although they are unlikely to fruit in the home. Many people grow jasmine and hibiscus as flowering plants without realizing that these flowers are quite useful in herbal teas; I have also made wine from the flowers of my bonsai jasmine and hibiscus specimens. While not technically edible, aromatic tropical trees like camphor, New Zealand tea tree, and eucalyptus can be grown as bonsai and provide a useful harvest. Furthermore, many unusual tropical fruits that are little known outside of their native areas could be experimented with as edible bonsai. I recommend experimenting with what you find locally, or seeking out any variety that captures your imagination. With the vastness of the Internet to search for unique varieties, the possibilities are endless.

Bonsai plants have a reputation for being very easy to kill and hard to grow, and for requiring a lot of time-consuming, detailed work. People are afraid to prune the tops of their plants, much less trim the roots of their valuable aged specimen. People who are afraid to prune their houseplants end up with long, spindly stems reaching for the ceiling with a little tuft of foliage on top. Pruning such a plant in order to produce a pleasing shape is easy, and creates a stronger, more stable plant. This is not much different from shaping a plant as a bonsai. When a plant is intended to produce a crop, some considerations may be different from traditional bonsai practice, outweighing ideals like always maintaining a perfect shape. Larger, fuller crowns are needed for a good-sized crop, making the sparser, heavily pruned style of bonsai unsuitable if production is important. Some desirable fruiting specimens, including the large-fruited citrus varieties like full-sized lemons, limes, oranges, and grapefruit, have leaves that are larger than would be desired in a more traditional bonsai style.

In traditional bonsai, the ideal specimen has a pot that is no deeper than the diameter of the bonsai's trunk. Striving toward this "perfection" leads to most bonsai being sold in very shallow trays that are difficult to keep watered in homes with

This seventy-inch-tall lemon tree bends under the weight of its twenty-seven lemons.

heaters and dehumidifiers—a problem that is compounded in dry climates. Especially when growing a large indoor bonsai specimen that might reach several feet in height, a larger, deeper pot than is traditional must be used to keep the plant healthy and productive. Root pruning—a requirement for training a tree that might grow over fifty feet tall in its natural environment to be an eighteen-inch specimen when it is 250 years old—also seems to be a sticking point for many potential bonsai enthusiasts. Pruning for this type of bonsai, as described in much bonsai literature, may involve washing all the dirt from the roots just before the tree breaks its dormancy in the spring and

Small roots were pruned in the process of exposing the base of the trunk and shaping the root ball of this strawberry tree.

The original soil level can still be seen on the trunk of this strawberry tree.

pruning a third of them before returning it to the same pot with fresh soil. This is very intimidating to the novice.

Most of the varieties discussed in this book are shrubs and small trees that are easy to keep in shape just by pruning the tops, although you sometimes have to let the tops get a little wild and wooly in flowering and fruiting season. Most of these tropical plants do not go dormant (edible figs are an exception) and cannot survive such harsh treatment as washing all the dirt from the roots. Like most typical houseplants, repotting involves gently disturbing the roots to stimulate growth into the new soil in a slightly larger pot. Sometimes roots at the base of the trunk are pruned and exposed to simulate aging and give the bonsai character. Because larger and deeper pots are used than with traditional bonsai, harsh root pruning is seldom required. Lightly pruning the foliage at the same time as repotting allows the plant to stay in balance with the disturbed roots, preventing it from going into shock before the new hair roots begin to grow and nourish your bonsai specimen.

Light requirements are another consideration in some situations. Most flowering and fruiting tropical varieties in this book require bright light to do their best; they may not produce if they don't receive enough light. Edible figs actually do much better outside during the summer. When they go dormant and lose all their leaves for a couple months in the winter, figs do just fine in a lower-light situation, or even a basement or garage kept above freezing, until they start to sprout new leaves again in the spring and once again need brighter light. Citrus plants are also happier outside in the summer, but in climates with cloudy and colder winter conditions, these light-loving bonsai specimens may need supplemental lighting. Inexpensive full-spectrum plant light bulbs that screw into normal sockets or even track lighting can be found in any large hardware or lighting store. Even a single 150-watt bulb can make a huge difference when providing supplemental light for a large specimen during low-light seasons.

Most people believe bonsai need constant daily misting in addition to other the time-consuming work required to keep bonsai. This myth was spread by workers at garden centers, who hoped that constant misting would keep little juniper bonsai alive longer indoors, or at least keep foliage soft enough that it would take a while for the bonsai enthusiast to realize the tree was really quite dead. I observed this behavior during thirty-five years of plant industry work while managing four large garden centers and operating my own wholesale bonsai business for twenty years. In fact, daily misting will benefit a bonsai for a week or so after repotting, since the disturbance to the roots hampers the plant's ability to draw water from the soil. This is especially true in dry climates and when repotting is done during warm weather. Outside this period, however, the varieties described in this book have no need for daily or even regular misting (although any specimen that will live for years will benefit and look better after being rinsed in the shower or outside with a hose a couple of times a year).

Another myth about bonsai is the belief that maintaining a bonsai speci-men requires hours of detailed work and pruning on a regular basis. This is a complete misconception. Traditional outdoor bonsai grow so slowly that some varieties are only pruned once a year, and in cold climates are put into cold storage with minimal care for the entire winter. Fast-growing tropical bonsai need to be pruned several times a year; this can be seasonal depend-ing on fruiting patterns. An edible fig can grow a three-foot shoot in a couple months during the spring, during which period it may be pruned a couple of times and then left alone until it goes dormant the next winter. Even fast-growing herbs don't need to be pruned more than once every month or two, although if a perfectly groomed specimen is desired, herbs need much more detailed work than slower-growing tropical bonsai or the traditional decidu-ous or evergreen outdoor bonsai. Because herbs grow so quickly compared to most tropical plants, and their leaves age and yellow in a much shorter time, they need to be pruned more often. A neglected herbal bonsai can show a lot of yellow leaves that are just a natural part of aging. Simply combing the foliage with your fingers will remove most of these leaves; the last few can be removed individually when grooming the herbal specimen for display.

Growing indoor bonsai that produce an edible crop doesn't have to be difficult. Water a couple times a week, fertilize once a month, prune a cou-ple times a year, repot every couple of years, add supplemental lighting if needed, and harvest your bonsai crop when ready. The varieties discussed in this book will grow in typical potting soils—no need for special bonsai mixes designed for evergreens and deciduous trees. Miniaturizing giant out-door trees over decades and centuries requires very limited use of fertilizers, but indoor tropical varieties grow year round and need regular feeding. As a rule, most commonly available fertilizers used at recommended strength will work just fine with these bonsai, although some varieties will prefer more acidic fertilizers.

Growing indoor fruiting bonsai is much easier than it sounds and can be very rewarding. Many people have sprouted citrus seeds and grown spin-dly trees that seldom produce fruit; by using the proper varieties and giving them the correct conditions, a surprising quantity of citrus fruit can be produced even in northern climates. Despite bonsai's reputation for being difficult to grow and keep alive, anyone who is even moderately successful at growing common houseplants should be able to grow spectacular indoor tropical bonsai that can produce a usable crop. Many plant owners cultivate the same few varieties of common houseplant that have no use beyond their ability to cleanse the air and provide a pleasant atmosphere in the home. The primary difference between these common houseplants and edible varieties trained as bonsai is that flowering and fruiting varieties as a rule need bright light, and thus may require supplemental lighting. The number of potentially useful and edible varieties of tropical plants that can be trained as bonsai is large, making possible a distinctive display of green plants unlike those in most homes. Furthermore, serving a guest produce from a beautiful houseplant can add a unique dimension to your hospitality, and makes for a very rewarding experience.

CHAPTER 2

Creating Instant Bonsai

The easiest way to start your edible bonsai collection is to visit a garden center and purchase an already-created bonsai from one of the varieties commonly used in the bonsai trade. Australian cherries, dwarf pomegranates and Natal plums should be easy to find this way. They will be small, like traditional bonsai, and won't bear heavily until they get some age and size. The garden center may also have "bonsai starters," which are less expensive partially shaped trees in four- to six-inch pots. These groomed starters, which need a minimum of pruning and often have large roots to expose upon repotting, can be planted in nice pottery and will look good immediately.

Depending on the size and quality of your local garden center and the area where you live, some of the varieties discussed here may be available as nursery stock plants in one-, two-, or five-gallon nursery pots. Australian cherries, pomegranates, olives, myrtles, figs, rosemary, and citrus are widely available in larger pots even in colder climates where they aren't planted outside as nursery stock. Plants ordered through the Internet will likely be young and small, allowing you to develop desired shapes as they grow. Most herbs and scented geraniums will be in pots no larger than six inches or one gallon, although they grow quickly and can be shaped in any direction you choose.

Many bonsai guides offer strict instructions for shaping different bonsai with specific forms, keeping them as diminutive as possible. This book changes the parameters, presenting bonsai that are larger than usual and pruning times and patterns that are directed toward production of meaningful crops. Some may be satisfied with a symbolic crop from a classic bonsai, but this book considers production of a useful crop to be an important part of the bonsai experience. It also focuses on creating larger bonsai than is typical in order to maximize production.

The best way to accomplish this goal is to purchase a good-sized nursery plant and "carve" an instant bonsai. It is usually easy to find good-sized blooming or fruiting citrus plants in five-gallon nursery pots. These can be minimally shaped and repotted into nice pottery, giving you an impressive specimen with a couple hours' work. The first edible fig plant I trained as a bonsai was a nursery "standard" in a five-gallon pot, delivered as a two-foot-diameter ball of foliage atop a forty-eight-inch stem. I let the plant grow and bear a first crop of figs that first summer. When it went dormant in the fall, I took a saw to the stem two feet above the ground, leaving an unbranched stubby trunk. When it sent out new shoots in the spring I left the ones I wanted and pinched them several times. The tree grew a nice shape that summer and bore figs again. After another year of growing and pinching tips, that fig bonsai has a full crown that is quite impressive in the summer and bears a large crop of figs. Taking a large older plant and cutting it back dramatically can be the quickest way to create a spectacular bonsai in a relatively short period of time. Besides figs, I've also done this with guavas, citrus, Natal plums, and Australian cherries. Some of these were left with two-inch diameter stubs and essentially no foliage, yet grew out a nice crown over the next year with regular pruning.

Although it may not be as dramatic, a nice nursery plant can often be pruned heavily, removing a third to more than half of the plant's branches and foliage, to create a beautiful bonsai immediately. This is where it is important to have a selection of plants to choose from, so you can select the inner structure that will create the best bonsai. In addition to a good main trunk, the ideal bonsai should have a nice main branch to one side some distance above the ground. It should be balanced by another branch, slightly higher up on the opposite side, for balance. A third branch should grow from the back of the bonsai, providing depth. These branches should come from different spots on the trunk rather than from the same original leaf node. The lowest branch should be the thickest, with each succeeding branch being a little smaller. Branches that project across the front, crossing the trunk and obscuring the inner bonsai, should be removed. Of course, it is unlikely that a large nursery plant will have this perfect shape, but hopefully you have picked out something with good enough balance and shape to give you something to work with. The three plants illustrated in this chapter were purchased at a local garden center in Fort Collins, Colorado, near my mountain home. The store offered a selection of six strawberry trees, a dozen myrtle-leaved oranges, and about thirty Key limes for me to choose my specimens from.

Citrus can be very easy to shape as bonsai. The large Key lime shown here was about forty inches tall in a three-gallon pot. It had just finished blooming and had some pea-sized fruits. It was easy to see the future shape in this plant even before anything had been trimmed. Only five growing tips were cut back, leaving the height of the specimen thirty inches from ground level when finished.

The tallest growing tips were pruned when shaping the crown of this Key lime bonsai.

Removing a strong branch that was too low on the trunk of this tree.

Fresh soil being added when potting the trimmed Key lime bonsai.

More than a dozen small, stubby, or spindly shoots were removed from the bottom half of the tree. A few that could have been removed were left because they carried small fruits. These would be removed after fruiting to better expose the open branch form. The foliage crown was pruned from the bottom up, exposing the bonsai structure, and the tips were pinched to fill out the top of the crown. One thicker branch was removed from below the main fork to open up the bonsai, allowing a good view of the flowing symmetry of the two main branches.

The front of the nursery tree in the photo became the rear of the finished bonsai, showing the scar where the branch was removed. The marks where some other branches were removed are visible; they will darken and scar over with age. Because not much foliage needed to be removed from this specimen, the root ball was reduced very little. I exposed a little less than one inch of trunk stem and just roughed up the edges of the root ball, adding some

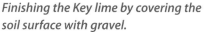

Finishing the Key lime by covering the soil surface with gravel.

Completed Key lime bonsai. This specimen is thirty inches tall.

fresh soil in a pot big enough to give the bonsai some room to grow.

If you look closely, you can see I lost some small Key limes with that larger branch, but it needed to be removed to look good, and there are other fruits on the specimen. The left-flowing movement of the two main branches is pleasing to the eye and is balanced by the foliage to the right, even though the two main branches cross each other slightly. It may not have the "perfect" shape, but it's still a very attractive bonsai with strong branches, a nice full crown, and a crop of small Key limes. Less than one month after shaping, this bonsai had new flower buds opening. After dressing the soil surface with fine pea gravel, I placed a snow-capped-mountain rock behind the bonsai to draw attention through the plant, giving an illusion of depth with a mountain in the distance.

The myrtle-leaved orange specimen shown here was twenty-four inches tall in a one-gallon nursery pot, and was covered with clusters of little

Pruning leaves and small branches from a myrtle-leaved orange tree.

Using a pointed bamboo stick to remove soil and expose the roots of the newly carved bonsai.

oranges. The crown didn't need to be cut back to obtain a nice shape, which was a good thing because there were orange clusters on the branch tips. One larger branch was removed from below the main fork, and a few oranges went with it, although there are several dozen left on the bonsai. A number of short branches and leaves were removed to expose the trunk and branch structure and to define the lower limit of the crown.

During repotting, a sharpened bamboo stick was used to loosen soil around the roots and base of the tree, exposing almost two inches of trunk that had been below the soil.

A few small roots were removed when exposing the trunk, but the rest of the root ball was only slightly disturbed. The tree was then planted with

Fresh soil should be tamped down around the root ball when potting. The original soil level can be seen on the trunk.

The completed myrtle-leaved orange bonsai is twenty-four inches tall.

some fresh soil in a pot large enough for it to grow in for a of couple years.

Exposing the trunk added to the height of the bonsai, and though the top was not pruned, the finished specimen rises twenty-four inches above the soil level. The added trunk length places the first branch at a nice interval above the ground and adds to the aesthetic effect of the curving flow in the trunk and branches of the bonsai. The soil surface was dressed with pea gravel, then topped with a multi-colored agate chosen to reflect the curve of the trunk and balance the "empty" side of the bonsai.

The strawberry tree shown here was about twenty-six inches tall in a one-gallon nursery pot, and had flowers and buds in several of the growing tips. Although it took off a large cluster of flowers, the tallest growing tip

Opposite page, top left: This strawberry tree has been removed from its pot and is ready to be trimmed.

Opposite page, top right: The bottom branches have been pruned, and the tall growing tip was removed.

Opposite page, bottom left: The strawberry tree is now ready to place into a bonsai pot.

Opposite page, bottom right: Fine pea gravel is used to cover the soil surface after the bonsai is potted.

Right: Strawberry tree bonsai. This specimen is twenty-two inches tall.

was removed just above the point where three nice branches were sprouting, bringing the crown of the bonsai into balance. More pinching will be needed to develop the crown, but as the tips were producing clusters of buds, they were left to grow, flower, and hopefully produce fruit before trimming. About half an inch of trunk and a large root were exposed when shaping the root ball before repotting, giving the finished bonsai a height of twenty-two inches above the soil level.

The bonsai was placed in the pot just to the left of center to balance the right-flowing movement in the tree's structure. Leaves and small branches were removed from the bottom up to shape the lower level of the crown. Two large branches were removed, one of which was below the large first limb left on the bonsai. The scars from removing those branches are visible, but will fade over time. Even with this harsh treatment, one month later the remaining buds were progressively blooming; the oldest flowers left on the bonsai had dropped, leaving clusters of tiny strawberry fruits growing in their place.

After the surface was finished with pea gravel, a piece of black obsidian collected in Oregon was selected to accent the bonsai. The rock was placed to anchor, balance, and reflect the flowing movement of the trunk and main flowering branch. The obsidian was particularly chosen for the contrast of its black color against the white flowers and pottery; it also reflects the color of the wingtips and neck of the sacred crane painted on the pot. The beautiful painted pottery also contrasts well with the bright green leaves and red trunk of the strawberry tree bonsai.

When creating these "instant" bonsai, the root ball usually cannot be flattened enough to fit in a conventional shallow bonsai pot. Like their crowns, the roots of traditional bonsai need years of training to be worked into shallow containers. The pots may depart from tradition in other ways, as well. Solid-colored earth-tone pottery is the customary choice for evergreen trees, while brightly colored or painted pottery is acceptable for flowering bonsai. These days, however, people are more concerned with whether the pottery style and color matches their home décor than its suitability for the bonsai. If we are pursuing this art to please ourselves, rather than feeling forced to follow tradition, the pottery style and color should reflect the artist's preferences. Some may prefer to choose each individual pot to match the bonsai, while others may want every pot in their bonsai collection to match.

Although it is not as fast as carving an instant bonsai, another way to create a bonsai is to plant an inexpensive small plant such as a fast-growing herb, scented geranium, or hot pepper directly in the ground. This technique has been used in traditional bonsai with outdoor trees, which are planted in the ground and encouraged to grow rapidly for several years. A fifteen-foot tree would be dug up and cut back to less than two feet, providing a thick trunk on which to develop a crown. By adapting this technique to fast-growing plants, a bonsai can be created in a single growing season.

Ideally this should be started in spring, at the beginning of the best growing season. Field-planting directly in the ground in a space with good soil and ample available water will encourage rapid growth. I have taken a four-inch pot of rosemary, like those available in any good garden center, and field-grown a plant that produced a bonsai under two feet tall with a one-inch diameter trunk in a single summer growing season. This can also be done in a large pot while pushing growth with lots of water and fertilizer. You won't get as much growth as is possible in the field, but it will be easier and less risky to move to a smaller pot when carving your large herb back into a bonsai. Field-growing and digging a plant carries some risk of losing the plant if conditions are too harsh, or if the root and crown pruning are not balanced. For this reason, I recommend growing several plants to train as bonsai. You may lose one or two, but an extra bonsai or three—especially a desirable herb—always makes a great gift.

Most of these fast-growing varieties put out many more new sprouting branches than will be needed to develop the bonsai structure. Your young plant should be cut back to a basic skeleton of a bonsai, with just the trunk and a couple of main branches pruned where you wish them to branch again. All extraneous new shoots and branches should be removed. As your bonsai-in-training grows, all new shoots on the trunk and main branches should be removed regularly except for the new branches forming at the tips of the pruned "skeleton." These new branches should be pinched at the point where you wish them to branch again. Don't be too obsessive about this process. Two to four pruning sessions through the summer should be enough. The point is to push lots of growth in the direction desired while keeping the plant from using too much of its energy developing unwanted branches. This process will work well even with little or no trimming through the growing season, although one good trim mid-season can make a big difference in the final shape. Refrain from pruning for the last month or two of the growing season before it is time to dig your specimen and replant it.

Digging a field-grown plant is necessarily a harsh procedure, likely causing root damage and reducing the plant's ability to take in water for several days as root tips redevelop. This is ideally done at the end of the growing season in cool weather, before the first frost. Avoid digging field-grown plants or repotting in hot weather, which will stress the plant too much. Your transplanted bonsai should kept out of the sun in a shady place to prevent it from drying it out before new roots develop. You will need a rather deep pot. You may want to consider using a training pot, like a ten-inch or two-gallon plastic nursery pot, for six months or so before moving your bonsai into nice display pottery.

In order to balance the unavoidable root damage when digging your field-grown bonsai, a large amount of foliage in the crown must be removed. As plants lose moisture through their leaves, enough foliage must be removed to balance the damage done to the roots. All growing tips should be removed. Some may be cut back severely depending on the seasonal growth and desired bonsai shape. Lower foliage, especially large leaves, should be removed from the bottom up to define the lower part of the crown. Expect to remove about half or more of the plant's leafy foliage to keep it in balance as it recovers from potting. These plants grow quickly enough to recover rapidly, and can look very good after just another month or two of growing in a pot.

If you purchase your potential bonsai through mail order or over the Internet—which may be the only way to obtain some of the more unusual tropical varieties like guavas or green tea, depending on your location—you will probably get a small, young plant. My green-tea bushes arrived as single-stem unbranched rooted cuttings six inches tall. In developing a small tropical plant as a bonsai, the best results will be obtained by pushing its growth in a good-sized pot for a year or more with only minimal shaping before cutting it back. Over a period of several years, this will create a thicker trunk and a more dramatic appearance than restricting your bonsai-in-training to a small pot with more frequent pruning within that same time span.

Of the many ways to create your edible bonsai, the easiest but least satisfying is to purchase one already created. Perhaps the best way is to find a large nursery plant and carve an instant bonsai. Explore the recesses of your local nurseries. Talk to the greenhouse manager about your interests. Search online if you can't find your desired variety locally. In more than twenty years of business, I've created tens of thousands of edible bonsai using the techniques described here, yet I am always on the lookout for new varieties and sources to explore.

CHAPTER 3

Bountiful Bonsai
Possibilities

T here are many species and varieties of edible and useful plants that can be trained as bonsai. Traditional concepts of bonsai can be put aside to allow for varieties that have leaves or fruit much too large to have been considered acceptable through the long history of this art form. While most people think bonsai are miniature trees that couldn't possibly bear enough fruit to be worthy of more than a symbolic harvest, even strict traditionalists in the art will consider and create bonsai up to six feet tall. To get a useful harvest from a bonsai, larger plants are a must—perhaps beyond six feet in height if the available space, the plant's characteristics, and the artist's desires make it suitable. The tree is still being shaped artistically and confined to a pot that is smaller than the chosen species would be allowed its natural habitat, growing in the ground.

While traditional bonsai are governed by artistic forms with strict guidelines, this book focuses on production of a useful harvest, which may prove a more important consideration than achieving the perfect artistic form of the tree. I personally have a difficult time removing a branch that is flowering or bearing fruit in order to improve the artistic shape of the tree. If I decide a branch must be removed for the long-term benefit of the bonsai's shape, the pruning is postponed until after the harvest. There are no strict guidelines here. Everyone has different concepts and preferences as to what artistic perfection and bountiful harvests mean to them. Let these guide your direction to manifest the type of bonsai you wish to grow. Just as it is possible to train a bonsai for years or even lifetimes, one can also use a harvest to create products like jams, jellies, and canned fruits, or even teas, dry herbs, or wines that can be stored and savored for many years. It's possible to freeze each year's harvest over two or three years until you have enough volume to ferment a small batch of wine. My collection includes edible bonsai that have been in my training for over twenty years, and there are wines created from bonsai harvests in my cellar that are more than twenty years old. While displaying a bonsai that one has trained for twenty years is very satisfying, there's nothing quite like the satisfaction of pouring someone a twenty-year-old glass of wine from the same bonsai that's on display.

My focus here is mostly on tropical and Mediterranean plant varieties which are active year-round, although some species may have dormant periods even when grown indoors. These varieties may thrive outside year-round in some climates, but they all can be grown entirely indoors under proper conditions. I have grown and shaped all the varieties discussed here, although not all of them have produced a harvest for me. Some, like avocados, may never produce fruit when grown indoors, but can do so when grown outdoors in a suitable climate. I have collected and experimented with edible and useful varieties for several decades, and I'm always looking for new varieties to try. While I expect most people to choose varieties that appeal to their taste, few sources will have the wide variety discussed here. Be open to the possibility of experimenting with species that are new or unfamiliar to you.

Australian cherry (*Eugenia myrtifolia*) Also known as brush cherry, this species has become widely used for indoor bonsai and is easily available in most locations. My bonsai nursery has sold more Australian cherries than any other species I grow. There are several varieties that make extremely attractive bonsai, including the miniature version most commonly found in shops and other sources that supply bonsai materials. One drawback to this miniature variety is that it seldom flowers, and when it does, it has only a few scattered blossoms. In twenty years of working with miniature Australian cherries, I have never seen a single fruit develop on them. There are also dwarf and standard varieties with larger leaves that flower reliably and often fruit very heavily. These larger varieties can be found in many locations and are often used for big topiaries, though their internode distance and overall size makes them less commonly used as bonsai. I see them most often as large double- or triple-ball topiaries up to six feet tall in local nurseries. Their

This dwarf Australian cherry, started from a five-gallon nursery plant, is now full of flower buds. This specimen is forty-six inches tall.

blooming season in my area is between June and September, with the heaviest period of flowering occurring in August. The bright pink cherries are really a type of berry rather than a true stone cherry; they're not exactly a sweet, juicy, delectable fruit. Though edible, they can be a little dry and mealy, and are better used for cooking or drying and adding to teas rather than eating fresh. While Australian cherries might not be your first choice if harvesting succulent fruit is your objective, they can be used to create the most spectacular "traditional" bonsai of any variety discussed in this book, with the added bonus of edible fruit. This species does very well indoors with bright light; their biggest requirement is lots of water. In fact, they are difficult to overwater if they have good drainage and bright light. It's best to use a larger pot than suggested for traditional bonsai so the soil doesn't dry out quickly.

Avocado (*Persea americana*) While many people have grown plants from avocado pits, they may not have done so with creating bonsai in mind. Avocados are quite easy to start: simply insert three toothpicks around the circumference of the pit and half-submerge it in a glass of water. The pit will split and send out roots and a green shoot that can grow for several months in water before being transferred to soil and a pot. The shoot should be pinched to make the plant branch as desired, and can be shaped like any other bonsai. Avocados have large leaves, and are best developed as a large-specimen bonsai so the leaves won't look so out of place. The literature says avocados seldom or never fruit indoors, and my experience backs this up. I have started and grown several with no success at fruiting, but someone in a suitable climate like California may be able to grow one outdoors and produce fruit successfully. At the very least, avocados are a cheap and easy way to start a potentially edible bonsai, and can be a great way to introduce a child to growing plants and shaping a tree.

Bahama berry (*Nashia inaguensis*) Bahama berry, also called pineapple verbena, is a small tropical woody herb with tiny bright-green leaves and a strong fragrance often described as a pineapple-vanilla blend. It blooms freely with tiny white flowers, and can develop orange berries that make a great addition to teas. Bahama berry has become popular for use as bonsai and can often be found at bonsai shops. Like other herbs, it is a fast grower, gets root-bound quickly, and requires plenty of pruning. If grown indoors, it will need very bright light and plenty of water.

Barbados cherry (*Malpighia glabra*) Barbados cherry, also called acerola, is a subtropical tree widely grown for its attractive flowers and ornamental fruit. Though sour, the fruit has good flavor and is used in jams, juices, wines, and baby foods. It is grown commercially as the best organic source of vitamin C. The leaves can be used for herbal teas.

Barbados cherries are a popular subject for bonsai and should be easy to find. Nurseries in milder climates will likely have larger specimens that can be carved into bonsai that will bear fruit right away. Barbados cherry is fairly easy to grow with well-drained soil and regular watering. Its vitamin C content alone makes it worth cultivating.

Basil (*Ocimum basilicum*) Most people are familiar with basil as a soft herb used in cooking that wouldn't seem to be a good candidate for bonsai. While basil might not survive as a bonsai for long enough to pass down through the generations, it is a woody shrub that can survive for years in the right conditions. My dinner last night included fresh basil from a bonsai specimen that is currently thriving in its second winter in my Colorado greenhouse. Basil requires bright light and warm temperatures to do well. Without the use of a greenhouse or solarium in cooler or northern climates, it will need a bright south or west window through the winter, and would benefit greatly from the addition of a spotlight-type full-spectrum plant light that supplies both heat and light. There are many varieties of basil; the smaller-leaved specimens like bush basil (*O. basilicum minimum*) make the most attractive bonsai. Standard sweet basil, as well as the exotic and fragrant lemon, lime, and cinnamon basils, are a good compromise between wanting a perfect small bonsai specimen and harvesting a large crop. Opal basil, with its beautiful purple leaves, can make a spectacular bonsai. Fast-growing herbs like basil are perhaps the most useful of all edible bonsai: one nice specimen can provide a fresh harvest for use in cooking several times a week. Basil should definitely be pruned back when it develops flowering spikes. Because it grows very quickly in good conditions, it can sometimes get out of hand and lose its bonsai shape. But it can be cut back sharply, even to solid wood, and will sprout out again to form a new shape and provide a continual harvest. Basil stems can get quite woody with age, making this a uniquely different, beautiful, and useful bonsai.

Bay laurel (*Laurus nobilis*) Sweet bay leaf, commonly used in the kitchen, comes from a large, slow-growing shrub that is quite attractive. One specimen can easily provide all the leaves needed, even for a cook who uses them often. Every pruning will provide leaves that can be dried and stored for long periods until needed in the kitchen. Like many other species, sweet bay will often send out side shoots or suckers from low on the trunk; these need to be pruned away along with the growing tips of the specimen. While bay leaves are used to flavor foods, they are

This thirty-inch sweet bay laurel has been in training for twelve years; it was started from a five-gallon nursery pot.

fibrous and indigestible—in fact, the strong rib in the leaf can actually be dangerous if it pierces the wall of a digestive organ. Tender young side shoots shorter than an inch or two can be consumed without this danger, offering many new possibilities in the kitchen.

Black olive (*Olea europeae*) Olive trees are highly desired ornamental trees in many locations, and also provide commercial olives and oils for the table. Black olives are widely available at commercial nurseries, although these ornamental varieties are generally non-fruiting. Many people who want olive trees seem to have no interest in harvesting and using the fruit, perhaps hoping to avoid the mess of unwanted fruit dropping in their yard. My experience with these ornamental non-fruiting varieties is primarily as a staple in my wholesale bonsai nursery business. Olives tolerate dry conditions in the home very well and are easy to grow, though somewhat slow to develop. It will take repeated pruning over time to develop a nice crown, but at a young age the trunk begins to develop the characteristic gnarled, knobby bark that makes the black olive an attractive bonsai specimen. The non-fruiting varieties, which have long, pointed silver-green leaves and occasionally produce small yellow flowers, are gaining wider use in traditional bonsai circles, and can often be found in bonsai collections at nurseries that carry a good selection of indoor bonsai. Be aware there is also another species with shiny rounded green leaves, the Florida black olive (*Bucida buceras*), which is often called black olive and is sold in many bonsai collections. The two species are not related, and the seed capsules of the Florida black olive are inedible.

Blood orange (*Citrus sinensis*) In my experience, larger citrus varieties like oranges and grapefruit are more difficult and less productive than the smaller citrus varieties discussed here, but blood oranges have worked well for me. Blood oranges are an unusual and delectable fruit, and are spectacular when used in gourmet cooking. One of my all-time favorite recipes, described in Chapter 6, "The Bountiful Harvest," uses blood oranges. Large-fruited citrus like this will form larger trees, and will therefore require ample space and bright light. They may need supplemental artificial lighting

The fourteen fruits on this sixty-three-inch blood orange tree are nearly ripe.

through the winter, especially in northern climates. All citrus will benefit from outdoor conditions in the summer; letting bees help pollinate the flowers in late spring will increase fruit production. Most citrus plants bloom most heavily in early spring, but will have scattered flowers throughout the year, providing a delightful fragrance in the house.

Buddha's hand citron (*Citrus medica* var. *sarcodactylis*) The fruit of this unique citrus resembles a bright yellow hand full of fingers. It has no pulp or juice; it is usually solid all the way through. The fragrant fruit can be diced and used like citrus zest in a wide variety of foods. The Buddha's hand flowers in clusters during early spring and, in my experience, often drops small fruit that apparently did not get pollinated. Because the fruits are so desirable, I have worked hard to pollinate my specimens. I've tried hand pollination with a small paintbrush, and I've moved them outside on warm spring days to attract the first local bees to the

These blood oranges are ripe enough to eat, but with more time will develop a purplish mottling on the rind. The flesh will become sweeter, turning from orange to reddish-purple.

A Buddha's hand citron. This fruit is about nine inches long and six around.

flowers. While most flowers drop without producing, I usually manage to get a few fruits to grow. My best year produced nine fruits from three specimens—enough to make two cases of wine and have some frozen to use in cooking for the next year. I love the name, flavor, and unique shape of this fruit, and my Buddha's hand bonsai is one of the most prized specimens in my collection.

Calamondin orange (× *Citrofortunella microcarpa*) Calamondin oranges are a created hybrid, believed to be a cross between mandarin oranges and kumquats, whose origin is lost to history. They are not found in the wild. The entire fruit is edible: the peel is sweet and the pulp is sour. These fruits are commonly used as a garnish for drinks or cocktails, and are sometimes frozen before use. They are delightful in cooking—simply chop them whole, removing the seeds, and add them to any dish. They can also be made into marmalade or wine. Calamondins have smaller leaves and fruit than a full-sized citrus, and are more shrublike, making them ideal for growing as citrus bonsai. In my experience, calamondins are the easiest to grow of the dozen or so citrus varieties I have experimented with, and are by far the most prolific. They bear two crops a year for me, blooming in spring with a crop of ripe oranges before Christmas and flowering again around New Year's Day to produce another crop in the spring. These oranges are often given as gifts during the Chinese New Year, as Chinese tradition holds that oranges in the house bring health, abundance, and good fortune during the coming year. Calamondins will hang

Variegated calamondin oranges lose their variegation when they turn ripe. The golf-ball-sized fruits have an intense orange flavor, and can be used, peel and all, in many types of cooking.

Top: Ripe calamondin oranges show up nicely against this forty-two-inch-tall variegated bonsai.

Bottom: These ripe calamondins still show faint signs of their variegation. They will not turn the bright orange of calamondins from a green variety.

on the tree for several months after ripening without going bad, and are best "stored" on the tree until used, although they can also be frozen for use in cooking. Under proper conditions, a calamondin will bear ripe fruit to pick almost year-round, even in a cold climate like my Colorado mountain home. There is also a gorgeous yellow variegated variety that makes a spectacular bonsai. Even the fruit is variegated until it turns ripe. Because of its easy growth and prolific production, I would strongly recommend the calamondin as a first choice for anyone wishing to grow a citrus bonsai.

Camphor laurel (*Cinnamomum camphora*) Camphor is a large evergreen tree with attractive, deeply fissured bark and large leaves that produce essential oils used in culinary spices and medicines. Camphor is widely used in over-the-counter medicines, and the leaves can be crushed to release the camphor fragrance. While I wasn't impressed with the first young tree I received, which looked like a whip with giant leaves, I have found that after several years of pruning the camphor can

make a spectacular bonsai, with plenty of leaves to use for potpourri or medicinal steams. My oldest specimen flowered regularly, though it never produced berries. This is a fast-growing large tree that requires regular hard pruning to shape, but it will develop nicely, and the leaves will be smaller if a well-branched crown is produced.

Carob (*Ceratonia siliqua*) Carob, an evergreen shrub native to the Mediterranean region, is widely used in foods, and is often considered a substitute for chocolate. The leaf stems and new growth are a deep burgundy color that contrasts nicely with the shiny green leaves and brown bark. Carob also develops a gnarled root system at the base of the trunk that adds a distinctive aged character to the bonsai. Like most Mediterranean varieties, carob prefers well-drained soils, tolerates dry conditions, and is well suited to growing indoors in bright areas. My carob bonsai has been in training for over a dozen years and has yet to flower or bear seed pods, but is nonetheless a beautiful and unique specimen.

Top: Crushing the leaves of the camphor tree releases a strong camphor scent, recognizable in many over-the-counter medications. This sixty-five-inch tree with a four-foot-diameter crown has been in training for sixteen years.

Bottom: The impressive root structure on the camphor tree gives it great character and an aged appearance.

Above: This forty-eight-inch carob tree has been in training for about eight years. It was started from a one-gallon nursery stock plant.

Castilian guava (*Psidium guineese*)
Also known as Brazilian guava, this small herbaceous shrub native to Central and South America is considered an invasive weed in other parts of the world where it has become naturalized. The pale-yellow fruit is less than an inch long, with many small, hard seeds. My specimen has flowered heavily but only produced a few small fruits. Castilian guava has a light tan bark that peels and curls away from the trunk and large branches in thin sheets, adding a distinctive aged character to the

Above: Ripening Castilian guavas show a scale infestation that was treated after picking the guavas.

Left: This Castilian guava has been in training for a couple years from a small five-gallon nursery plant; it now has a few small fruits. This specimen is forty-three inches tall.

bonsai specimen. Bright light, well-drained soil, and frequent watering will keep a Castilian guava happy indoors.

Chilean guava (*Ugni molinae*) Chilean guava is a small shrub with deep green leaves on red twigs. It bears delicate pink bell-shaped flowers in spring, and forms delightful small fruits, less than half an inch in diameter, which are more like a sweet berry than other guavas. These are wonderful fresh as they ripen from pink to purple. The Chilean guava is the smallest of the guavas, and is easy to grow as a tabletop bonsai that can bear abundant, though small, fruit. The leaves are only one to two centimeters long, giving them a scale perfect for creating a more traditional bonsai that will flower and bear edible fruit. Like other members of the myrtle family, its leaves have a spicy scent when crushed. Chilean guava will grow well indoors as long as it doesn't get too hot; they prefer moist, well-drained soil and medium to bright light.

Chilean myrtle (*Luma apiculata*) Chilean myrtle is a very attractive shrub with small dark-green leaves that give off a spicy scent when crushed. Fragrant white flowers in early summer lead to edible bluish-black berries in the fall. The papery bright orange bark peels away from the creamy white underbark, creating a beautiful contrast on the trunk and main branches. This has always been one of my favorite bonsai for demonstrations, display, and sales. It produces enough foliage to offer a regular aromatherapeutic lift by picking and crushing a leaf. I would do this for anyone visiting my greenhouse, just to see the sparkle in their eyes when smelling the delightful fragrance. This alone would convince a skeptic of the value of aromatherapy! Easy enough to grow indoors in bright light, Chilean myrtles need plenty of water to support their numerous leaves. This is a great species for anyone wishing to grow a traditional-looking indoor bonsai that will produce abundant foliage and edible berries that are easy and fun to use.

Coffee (*Coffea arabica*) Coffee trees are easy to find, and grow well as houseplants. Like nearly everything else these days, online sources are a click away, but I have also found coffee trees as groups of about half a dozen seedlings in inexpensive four-inch foliage plant collections in flower shops and greenhouses throughout the United States. The plants can be separated easily at this stage or grown as a grove. They will grow quickly enough to develop a nice shape in a couple of years, and will be impressive even sooner

Though this forty-six-inch Chilean myrtle bonsai needs pruning, weeding, and a gravel finish, it bears fragrant mid-summer flowers.

At about four years old, this coffee tree grove is not yet ready to produce beans. This specimen is thirty-four inches tall.

as a grove. It may take a seedling three to five years to flower. My older specimens flowered regularly and produced a few beans. A large coffee bonsai can produce enough beans to bring great satisfaction to the grower, even though the harvest will never be significant. Even a single ceremonial tasting is a very rewarding way to expand the artistic experience of bonsai.

Costa Rican mint bush (*Satureja viminea*) This mint grows quickly into a very woody shrub with attractive fissured bark and small, round, bright lime-green leaves. Tiny white flowers bloom profusely along the stems on a regular basis. The plant contains high levels of menthol oil, the source of mint flavoring that is also used in many over-the-counter medicines. Barely brushing against the leaves will release a strong mint fragrance into the air. While this plant is widely grown and used in Costa Rica, it was only discovered and named in the latter part of the twentieth century; it is not listed in my 1976 edition of *Hortus Third*, the definitive dictionary of cultivated plants in the United States. When writing my book *Herbal Bonsai* (published in 1996), I tracked down a member of the expedition that discovered and named this plant, and learned that the local population cuts branches of it to place on coals under grilling meats. It is also used as a medicinal herb, primarily in teas, because of the menthol content. The Costa Rican mint bush grows very quickly and often sends out strong new shoots from the ground, roots, trunk, and large branches of the bonsai. These will grow much more vigorously than the growing tips of the tree and should be removed regularly, unless the artist wishes to dramatically change the shape of the bonsai. All of the lower shoots must be removed or the bonsai will quickly start to look like a multi-trunked bush instead of a miniature tree. A mint bush bonsai requires very bright light and lots of water. Being more of a woody herb than an actual tree, it will benefit from a larger pot with more soil than most other bonsai discussed here. It will also become pot-bound more quickly, necessitating more frequent repotting. Because of its fast growth and high menthol content, one medium-sized Costa Rican mint bush will likely produce as much mint flavoring as any family could use. The leaves can be used fresh or dried, and the stems—like those of many types of herbs—can be saved to soak in water and place on coals under foods being grilled. With its attractive appearance, bright lime-green leaves, and intense fragrance, this plant

This four-year-old Costa Rican mint bush, grown from a cutting, is now thirty-six inches tall. The leaves have a very strong mint fragrance.

often made the biggest impression on any of the visitors to my greenhouse. Unfortunately, it is not really produced on a commercial basis and may not be easy to find, perhaps because it attracts insect pests like white fly and aphids. Despite this, I consider Costa Rican mint bush a very desirable plant to grow, and it has a place of value in my collection.

Dwarf Lemon (*Citrus limon*) The earliest uses and cultivation of lemons are lost to history, but there are many varieties available today. Eureka lemons are the common grocery-store lemon; Lisbon lemons are very similar. Meyer lemons (*Citrus × meyeri*), a less acidic, round fruit derived from a cross between a lemon and an orange, have become very popular. All three of these varieties are widely grown as ornamentals and can be found in large garden centers everywhere. Ponderosa lemons, believed to be a natural cross between a lemon and a citron, bear large fruit with a bumpy rind that can weigh as much as a pound; they are used like regular lemons. A variegated pink lemon is also available, with attractive green-and-white foliage and a pink tinge to new growth. The fruit is similar to the common Eureka lemon except for the variegated rind that disappears as the fruit ripens; the pink flesh and juice inside, similar to regular lemons in taste, is a delightful surprise, and can be used to make natural pink lemonade. These beautiful citruses are becoming more common, as some of the large commercial ornamental plant growers have been distributing

Top: This seventy-inch lemon tree is struggling to bear the weight of its twenty-seven lemons.

Bottom: Ripe lemons ready to pick.

Top: This variegated pink lemon has been in training for a couple years. The forty-eight-inch specimen began as a five gallon nursery stock plant.

Bottom: This pink lemon was variegated before turning ripe. New flower buds can be seen developing on a lower branch.

them to nurseries all over the country as part of their citrus collections. Most lemons sold in nurseries are grafted onto vigorous citrus rootstocks that actually make for a stronger plant that is easy to grow, while also keeping the lemon tree growing as a dwarf rather than a large standard tree. Traditional bonsai artists may be horrified at using grafted trees, but we are breaking new ground here; most citrus rootstocks have thick trunks and nice large exposed roots that can add greatly to the character of the bonsai. New shoots or "suckers" will sometimes sprout from below the graft. These will look different from the upper growth and should be removed whenever they are seen. Besides detracting from the appearance of the bonsai, they will grow quickly, sapping strength from the desirable lemon-producing part of the tree. Lemons need bright light, and benefit from extra artificial lighting if winter conditions don't provide enough natural sunlight; they thrive outside during the summer. All of my citrus here in Colorado grows better and looks healthier when grown outside in the summer. A good dose of acid fertilizer can help the lemon tree stay healthy and produce a lot of fruit. A natural source of acidity, which citrus seem to love—though not a replacement for acid fertilizer—is some coffee grounds thrown on the surface of the their soil. When ripe, lemons can be left on the tree for a long time to be picked when needed. Along with the flowers, which are wonderfully fragrant, the myriad uses of fresh lemons make this one of the most desirable of all the edible bonsai. Given the right conditions, lemons are comparatively easy to grow and can be quite productive.

Dwarf lime (*Citrus aurantifolia*) Persian limes, similar in size to lemons, are found everywhere in markets. The most common variety, especially as an ornamental widely available in nurseries, is called Bearss seedless lime. The Key lime, also called a Mexican lime, is a small round lime with intense flavor that is well known and highly desirable for use in cooking and making beverages. Commercial Key lime trees are often grafted, but strong trees can be grown from a seed out of a store-bought Key lime. Kaffir lime (*Citrus hystrix*) is a small rough-skinned lime that is primarily grown for its leaves; it doesn't seem to fruit well when cultivated indoors. Lime leaves are used as medicine and as a culinary spice in many Southeast Asian cuisines. Most people are unaware that green limes are not completely ripe. If left on the tree long enough, limes will turn yellow, retaining the green color in the juice and pulp and growing sweeter as they ripen. All of the above-mentioned varieties are easy to find, and details of their care and growth are essentially the same as for lemon trees. Smaller Key limes, which have small leaves, can make a bonsai similar in scale to traditional bonsai. Limes are easy to grow, can be very productive, and make a great addition to any citrus bonsai collection.

Dwarf Pomegranate (*Punica granatum* var. *nana*) Dwarf pomegranate is a pretty shrub with small leaves. It flowers profusely in the spring and at other times of year with striking orange to red flowers. The plants develop fruit that average two to three inches in diameter; while small and not as juicy as standard full-sized pomegranates, they are edible. Standard pomegranates, which are not as easy to grow indoors, have large leaves and go dormant through the winter, even indoors. They can have spectacular flowers and produce full-sized fruit, but are not as suitable for bonsai cultivation as the dwarf variety. Dwarf pomegranates are fairly easy to find in well-stocked garden centers, and are generally a prominent component of indoor bonsai collections at these retail locations. Dwarf pomegranates will stay evergreen and flower often when kept in a warm environment. Exposure to temperatures near freezing will cause them to go dormant at least briefly, showing bright yellow "fall color" in the foliage and dropping all the leaves. With renewed warmth, however, they will sprout new green growth very quickly. The dwarf pomegranite is a good choice for anyone wishing to start growing edible bonsai, as they are easy to find and grow. They will reward the grower by producing flowers as well as fruit almost immediately.

This dwarf pomegranate, started from a five-gallon nursery stock plant, has been in training for a year and seven months. It is forty-two inches tall.

This close-up shows a nearly ripe dwarf pomegranate and a flower bud.

Edible Figs (*Ficus carica*) Edible figs are native to the Middle East, the cradle of civilization; they have been grown as a diet staple since before recorded history, and were likely the first plant to be intentionally cultivated. Fossilized figs have been found in Neolithic villages dated from before 9000 BCE, and figs are mentioned in the oldest literature. They hold a special place in the history of food culture and have long been considered a romantic, even erotic food to serve to a lover. There are many ornamental fig species, including the common *Ficus benjamina*, which is widely used for indoor landscaping and easily available everywhere. These shiny-leaved evergreen ornamental figs can also make nice bonsai, but they don't produce edible fruit. Edible figs have very large, dull leaves that are hairy underneath; they go dormant in the winter, even when kept in the greenhouse. Some cultivars can survive quite cold temperatures when dormant. The desirability of edible figs has given rise to elaborate strategies for helping them survive cold winters and bear fruit afterward: surrounding the entire tree with a mulch-filled cage; or digging a trench out from one side of the tree, severing half the roots on the opposite side, and laying the entire tree down into the trench to be covered with mulch. It seems much easier to just grow the fig in a large pot and move it to a protected space during the winter. Edible fig trees can grow very large, however, and will need yearly pruning to keep the size manageable for your available space. One of the best ways to train a fig bonsai is as a large patio tree, grown outside through the summer season and moved to a protected space such as a porch, garage, basement, or spare room while dormant in winter. Figs tolerate temperatures down to freezing at this time, and take up less space after the large leaves have dropped off. Edible figs thrive in hot weather. As long as your fig bonsai gets enough water, it will be happier outside in the summer than in the brightest window. Figs need a lot of water, especially when producing fruit, and will benefit from as large a pot as you can give them. It is nearly impossible to overwater an edible fig in a pot with good drainage; the fruit will not be as juicy if the tree is allowed to dry out between watering times. They can start bearing figs by mid-summer and will still be producing when the leaves drop for the winter. There are probably thousands of different fig cultivars, and they are grown everywhere in the world that the local climate permits. The varieties I've grown seem to be pretty similar in growth habits and general appearance. The difference is primarily in the fruit. The Brown Turkey variety is large, with a dark purplish-brown color when ripe. These figs mature much later than many other varieties and can often be found fresh in produce departments of good grocery stores when in season. Kadota is a white- or green-skinned fig with amber to salmon-colored flesh; it can produce from early summer into the fall. I found a similar variety called White Texan in Austin, Texas, but with a whitish blush to the fruit and a pale amber flesh. The Peter's Honey Fig is a yellowish-green fig with light golden-yellow flesh. When I was selling edible bonsai at the local farmer's market, the fig trees attracted more attention than citrus with ripe fruit. People would spot them from across the market and make a beeline for my display. When they saw that dramatic fig bonsai full of fruit, they inevitably wanted one of their own. Figs grow vigorously and can send out more than three feet of new growth in a single growing season if not pinched back. It should be noted, however, that pinching can delay or reduce fig production. Woody sections with at least two leaf nodes pruned from a mature tree can

Top: This Celeste edible fig is still in a plastic training pot after two years of training. This specimen is fifty inches tall from the surface of the soil.

Bottom: Close-up of a fig on the Celeste tree.

be readily rooted by dipping one end into rooting hormones and planting in a light potting soil. Young plants make a great gift and will often bear figs their first summer. Of course, if you get several, you may decide to keep them all and create your own orchard in moveable pots.

Eucalyptus (*Eucalyptus* sp.) There are well over five hundred species of eucalyptus, mostly native to Australia; various sources report from one to five hundred species currently growing in California. Apparently eucalyptus hybridizes easily and has a widely varying general appearance in both leaves and bark, yet many species closely resemble each other and are hard to differentiate. Flowers can be showy, but my specimens have never bloomed indoors. The main variety I've grown as bonsai, called peppermint willow (*Eucalyptus nicholii*), has narrow gray-green leaves that emit a strong peppermint fragrance when crushed. The large, hairy, teardrop-shaped leaves of the lemon eucalyptus (*Corymbia citriodora*), the source of citronella, have a strong lemon component in their essential oils; my specimens have developed elaborate twisted exposed roots. Eucalyptus oils, widely used in medicines, perfumes, and flavorings, are collected by boiling the leaves in water to distill the essential oils. Used in cough drops, decongestants, and other medicines, eucalyptus has a soothing effect on the respiratory system, and the leaves can be boiled uncovered on the stove to create a soothing steam as a room humidifier. Eucalyptus is perhaps the most useful tree on the planet. The wood is very hard when dry and has been used extensively in many kinds of construction, as well as for fuel. It grows so quickly that there is much interest in using various eucalyptus species for biomass production of fuels. Because they use a lot of water, eucalyptus trees have even been used in mass plantings to drain swampy areas harboring malarial mosquitoes. They need well-drained soil and should be watered heavily and frequently. While eucalyptus is more useful than edible, it makes an interesting addition to any bonsai collection.

Top: Green tea flowers are smaller than other camellias, but they are beautiful and prolific.

Bottom: This sixteen-inch green tea bonsai was shipped to me as a six-inch tall rooted cutting. I allowed several new shoots to develop to balance the strong flowing movement of the main stem, as well as to produce more foliage for harvesting.

Green tea (*Camellia sinensis*) Camellias, widely grown ornamental trees native to Southeast Asia that have long been prized for their showy flowers, were often featured in ancient Chinese paintings. After being introduced to England in the mid-eighteenth century, they became the most prized luxury flower in Europe until commercial orchids arrived on the scene. Several species of camellias are grown for their flowers, their seed oils, and the tea made from the leaves. The most significant, of course, is the green tea bush (*Camellia sinensis*) responsible for the drink that rivals coffee as the preeminent hot beverage around the world. White, green, and black teas are all produced from the same leaves by using different curing techniques. The finest teas are made from the tender new growth picked every couple of weeks, although I save every leaf when I prune my tea bushes. Ornamental camellias are known for having large, showy flowers that bloom in the dead of winter in Europe and North

America, which may explain their popularity. The green tea plant has small but pretty flowers less than two inches across, with white petals surrounding the camellia's trademark showy cluster of big yellow stamens. Ornamental camellias usually just bloom once, in midwinter, but the green tea plants in my house and greenhouse bloom all winter long. Preferring an acidic, well-drained soil, with frequent watering and bright light, the green tea plant can be shaped into attractive tabletop-sized bonsai that flowers frequently. Its useful harvest makes for a unique homegrown treat.

Hibiscus (*Hibiscus rosa-sinensis*) Tropical hibiscus is widely grown as an ornamental shrub, and is easy to find in garden centers and nurseries everywhere. It has large, shiny leaves and is known for its large, spectacular flowers in many colors. The edible flowers can be added to salads and are used for teas and other drinks, contributing color, flavor, and vitamins whenever they are used. Hibiscus flowers are also used in shampoos and other hair treatments. Drying and saving flowers from a good-sized hibiscus bonsai can produce plenty of useful material. Roselle (*Hibiscus sabdariffa*) is the species most widely used for consumption around the world and in commercial preparations. It is the fleshy calyx that surrounds and holds the petals, rather than the petals themselves, that is used in many kinds of hot and cold beverages. Roselle is not easy to find in plant form, but the seeds are available from some specialty companies. Tropical hibiscus plants are easy to grow and shape as attractive bonsai, and can be found in nearly every plant shop. There are some miniature varieties better suited to bonsai, and at least one miniature with variegated foliage and small flowers that can make a very striking bonsai specimen. Hibiscus bonsai thrive with rich soil, bright light, and ample water. They can get large, but will reward the grower with beautiful and useful flowers.

Hot peppers (*Capsicum* sp.) The bewildering variety of peppers found in gardens and markets everywhere are cultivated from five basic species—*C. annuum, C. frutescens, C. chinense, C. pubescens, and C. baccatum.* Peppers are native to the Americas, but have spread worldwide and now constitute an important part of the local cuisine in many countries. Almost every gardener has grown peppers, but few consider that they can be more than summer annuals. Peppers can grow as a woody shrub that will live for several years and produce peppers continually, even in winter. The small ornamental peppers available in flower shops everywhere are an obvious choice for bonsai; their dwarf stature and small leaves and fruit almost create a natural bonsai without much pruning. Many hot culinary peppers are not dwarf varieties, but still make nice bonsai if pruned and kept in check. Which variety is best depends more on the grower's culinary preference than the plant's dwarf characteristics. I've grown a number of them, including jalapeno, habanero, kung pao, cayenne, and a small red spicy pepper called Apache that's a new favorite. I've even wintered a pepper in a pot, planted it in the ground the following summer, and dug it back up for a second winter in a pot—although this is harder on the plant than just keeping it in a container full time. If the crown of a pepper bush gets leggy and droops, and doesn't have great shape, the bush can be pruned dramatically to thick wood and it will sprout and flower again very quickly. The main requirement for hot peppers to thrive is warm temperatures. I place them on an overhead shelf in my winter greenhouse, closer to the peak than the floor, to take advantage of the warmth up there when the sun is shining. Peppers will survive the winter in a bright sunny window, and benefit from the heat and additional light of a well-placed spotlight-type full-spectrum plant light. Rich potting soil and frequent fertilization will keep your pepper plants happy and productive. One problem with peppers is their tendency to attract insects, especially aphids, which tend to flourish under indoor conditions. The best way to deal with an infestation is to wash the plant with a high-pressure water spray and then spray it with soapy water to suffocate any insects that have survived the washing.

Jaboticaba (*Myrciaria cauliflora*) Jaboticaba is a small, slow-growing tree native to Brazil. Its attractive two-toned peeling bark and pale salmon-colored new growth, which turns into light-green leaves, have contributed to its recent popularity and availability for use as an indoor bonsai subject. A distinctive feature of jaboticaba is the one- to two-inch purple-black fruits resembling large grapes that form on very short stems directly off the trunk and main branches. These fruits are eaten fresh right off the tree, and do not keep long after picking. It is far more common to see them processed into jams, wines, liqueurs, and other foods than available fresh, except in local markets. Jaboticaba grows slowly and will take some time to produce fruit—anywhere from six to twenty years, according to various authorities. The specimen I've been training for five years has yet to flower. Jaboticaba is a graceful tree with delicate foliage that can make a beautiful classic bonsai, whether it fruits or not. A heavier soil full of mulch that can hold moisture is best for these water-loving trees. They are often flooded for weeks in their native habitat, and prefer a moist soil with frequent watering. The only problem I've observed with my jaboticaba bonsai is damage to the foliage if it dries out too much between watering periods.

This forty-one-inch jaboticaba started as a small tree shipped to me in a six-inch pot. It has been in training for five years.

Jasmine (*Jasminum* sp.) A number of jasmine species are grown ornamentally and commercially for their fragrant flowers. Angel-wing jasmine (*Jasminum nitidum*) is a medium-sized shrubby evergreen vine that produces an abundance of fragrant two-inch white pinwheel blossoms that pop out of purple buds. Though jasmine is supposed to be a summer bloomer, my twenty-year-old specimen blooms at Christmas and New Year every winter, and has more days with flowers than without in any given year. The fragrance of this species is less intense than other varieties, but my large-crowned six-foot specimen can be smelled throughout my living room when it is blooming freely. Star jasmine (*Trachelospermum jasminoides*) is a dwarf evergreen vine that blooms heavily once a year, with clusters of tubular five-petaled flowers that give off a strong jasmine scent. The fast-growing vine requires regular pruning, but will develop a nice trunk to make a beautiful small- to medium-sized bonsai. Common jasmine (*Jasminum officinale*) is the classic jasmine used for perfumes and aromatherapy since the beginnings of recorded history; the original native source is unknown. Summer-blooming and often deciduous, it has spread in cultivation everywhere it will survive. Tea jasmine (*Jasminum sambac*) is the source of jasmine flavor in jasmine teas. The fresh flowers are mixed with dried tea leaves, which absorb moisture and oils from the flowers. The flowers are often removed, but can be left in the dry tea and steeped all together. Tea jasmine grows as a medium-sized shrub, and is not a vigorous plant with fast-growing vines like other jasmines. Night-blooming jasmine (*Cestrum nocturnum*) is a member of the unrelated potato family. It has an intensely sweet odor which may cause some people to have a strong allergic reaction and difficulty breathing. It is reportedly toxic, and internal consumption is definitely not recommended. A large shrub with long leaves, night-blooming jasmine is difficult to shape as a classic bonsai, but the intense fragrance when the flowers open at dusk makes it an interesting plant to grow. All of the above-mentioned varieties should be readily available in local nurseries. Angel-wing, star, and tea jasmines are best suited for cultivation as indoor bonsai. I've had angel-wing and star jasmine bonsai in training for more than twenty years with good results. The star jasmine developed an interesting bark and trunk structure and filled the entire house with fragrance when it bloomed. My twenty-plus-year-old angel-wing jasmine bonsai is a large plant that fills a four-by-six-foot west window in my living room, making a bold statement when people enter my home, especially when it is blooming. It blooms heavily several times a year and produces enough flowers to use in tea and even to make a small vintage of two cases of jasmine-flower wine. Jasmines need bright light, but are easy plants to grow, and the flowers are very rewarding. The vining varieties require regular pruning. Any new shoots that emerge from the trunk, roots, or ground should be removed to keep the plant looking like a bonsai rather than a multi-stemmed bush.

Kumquat (*Fortunella* sp.) While some authorities classify the kumquat as *Citrus japonica*, most consider it to be a separate genus from other citrus. Kumquats, the smallest citrus fruit, are only one or two inches long. They have smaller leaves than large-fruited citrus varieties, making them ideal candidates for bonsai. Fresh kumquats can be found in produce markets in late fall and early winter. There are round and oval varieties; the oval nagami variety is most widely grown as an ornamental and for the fruit market. Kumquats have a sweet peel and sour flesh, and are mostly eaten fresh in their entirety. They are served as a garnish with food or drinks. Fresh kumquats may be chopped and used like citrus zest in many dishes. They also can be made into a unique marmalade or preserved by canning in sugar syrup. Although the fruit is small, kumquats can flower and fruit heavily, and a medium to large specimen can produce dozens or even hundreds of fruits. Kumquats are well suited to growing in containers. They do best in a rich soil full of humus that holds moisture well, as their natural habitat in China is along streams where the soil stays damp. Kumquats require more regular watering than other citrus, especially if restrained in a small bonsai

This kumquat, which began as a two-gallon nursery plant, has been in training for less than a year.

These kumquats will turn orange when ripe.

pot. They are more cold-tolerant than other citrus, including periods below freezing, and are suited for growing as a larger patio bonsai outside in milder climates. Most kumquats sold in nurseries are grafted, which can produce a thick trunk and impressive exposed roots that lend an aged character to the specimen. Spectacular variegated kumquats are also available that are easy to train as indoor bonsai. A variegated kumquat bonsai, full of fruit, would be the center of attention at any bonsai show.

Lavender (*Lavendula* sp.) English lavender (*L. angustifolia*), the widely grown lavender used commercially, is a cold-hardy species that needs to go dormant, and is not really suitable to grow as bonsai. Spanish lavender (*L. stoechas*) is a dwarf perennial shrub with attractive gray-green foliage and large pink to purple flower spikes. While this is the most attractive species of the group for bonsai, it is fussy and not as long-lived as other lavenders. French lavender (*L. dentate*) is a woody upright shrub with a more open growth habit, distinguished by the sharply toothed edges of its silvery green foliage. The leaves have a strong fragrance that is slightly different from that of traditional English lavender. While not often used commercially, French lavender can be used like other lavenders. I use it for potpourri, fresh aromatherapy, and as an added fragrance in teas. The oldest homemade wine in my cellar is actually French lavender wine from 1986. This is the best species to grow as bonsai because it is long-lived, grows into a nice upright shape, and can flower all year long. The crown of a mature lavender plant can become quite thick and droopy, with way too many growing shoots and older foliage in the interior of the crown that has turned brown or black. This can be prevented with regular pruning, or the bonsai can be cut back dramatically to solid wood, which will sprout quickly into a new crown. The small French lavender plants that can be found in the herb section of most well-stocked garden centers will grow rapidly into a small- to medium-sized bonsai. Small herbs like this can be planted in the garden in the spring and field-grown through a growing season before being dug up in the fall and pruned strongly. This technique can produce a dramatic bonsai with a thick trunk in a short period of time. French lavender is very tender and will not tolerate freezing temperatures. It likes well-drained soil and should be allowed to dry out between waterings, although not to the point of wilting. Like most herbs, it does best under full sun outside and a bright window indoors. French lavender also benefits from additional artificial lighting if kept indoors under low light conditions during the winter.

Lemon guava (*Psidium littorale*) Lemon guava is a small, fast-growing evergreen tree with attractive peeling bark. Its golf-ball-sized fruits, which have white flesh, small seeds, and yellow skin when ripe, are eaten fresh, used in cooking, and made into juice, jams, and jelly. The leaves are dried and used for tea in some areas. Guavas flower in spring and early summer and bear ripe fruit by August. That fall crop is the heaviest, but sparser flowers and fruit emerge at other times of the year. A lemon guava can get big for a houseplant, and is best trained as a six- to eight-foot specimen. Even at this size, it may occasionally need a severe pruning to keep it at a manageable size. I've pruned out-of-control specimens down to two-inch-diameter branch and trunk stumps, which immediately sprouted many shoots that with frequent pinching created a full crown. Guavas like well-drained soil, but will use plenty of water. The growing tips will quickly start to droop when the plant gets dry, and this is a reliable indicator of when to water. Of course, like any fruit-bearing tree, its fruits will taste best if ample water is given as they are growing. The lemon guava is relatively easy to grow and can produce unique and tasty fruit every year under good conditions. These fast-growing bonsai do best in a larger pot.

Lemon verbena (*Aloysia triphylla*, also *A. citriodora*) Some authorities put this plant, which is native to South America, in

Top: This lemon guava is still in a training pot six months after being dug up and cut back from an old plant that had rooted though its pot and into the ground. This specimen is eighty-four inches tall.

Bottom: A close-up view of ripe golf-ball-sized lemon guavas.

the genus *Lippia*. Lemon verbena is a fast-growing woody shrub that develops attractive gray furrowed bark with age. Its narrow, pointed, light-green leaves can go deciduous, and the plant will remain dormant for a period if subjected to cold temperatures near freezing or other shocks. Spikes of small white flowers erupt from lilac-colored buds in early summer. Lemon verbena is generally acknowledged as having the strongest, cleanest lemon fragrance of any of the lemon-scented herbs. Just brushing the leaves will release an intense lemon odor that can fill a room. Lemon verbena has extensive culinary uses, from flavoring meat (fish and poultry) dishes and sauces to sorbets and drinks; it is also very good blended with herbal or black teas. Fresh or dried leaves can be used anywhere lemon flavor is desired, though fresh leaves have stronger flavor than dried ones. The essential oils in this plant are strong antioxidants, and have been used medicinally as well as in fragrances and other cosmetics. Its scent has aromatherapeutic qualities, and lemon verbena tea has long been renowned for its soothing and relaxing effects on the body. Lemon verbena likes warm temperatures and can grow very quickly in suitable conditions, producing plenty of leaves for household use. This herb may have more potential uses around the house and kitchen than any other species discussed here, and is well worth growing as an edible bonsai. My oldest specimen has gone dormant several times and has sometimes died back to a stump that sprouts a new strong trunk. Lemon verbena can be kept to a nice tabletop size or allowed to grow into a medium-sized tree up to six feet tall. The top may die back dramatically if the tree goes dormant, but vigorous new growth can quickly create a new crown. Lemon verbenas need bright light, warm temperatures, and well-drained soil to thrive, and will take plenty of water when actively growing. Aphids, white flies, spider mites, and similar pests are attracted to this plant, and indoor infestations may become serious. In addition to regular soap sprays, moving the specimen outdoors, trimming away heavily infected growing tips, and washing with high-pressure water sprays can take care of the problem. Strong insecticides should not be used on any plant whose leaves will be consumed.

Limequats (*Citrus × japonica*) Limequats are a cross between Key limes and kumquats; the several varieties result from crosses with round and oval kumquats. One called Lakeland is crossed with a round kumquat, creating a small, slightly oval fruit, smaller leaves, and a more dwarf habit than other crosses. In my experience, the oval cross, sometimes called a Margarita limequat, is a more vigorous grower, with oval fruit nearly the size of a small egg that turn bright yellow when ripe. Limequats have

The perfect shape of this limequat has been sacrificed to maximize fruit production. The seventy-six-inch specimen now has nearly a hundred green fruits just beginning to ripen. Purchased as a six-foot-tall tree, it has been in training for five years.

Six weeks after the picture at left was taken, most of the fruit on this limequat bonsai have turned ripe and are ready to use. Ripe citrus always makes a striking specimen.

edible skin and lime-flavored green pulp and juice. Except for the seeds, limequats can be eaten whole, made into marmalade or wine, and added to many dishes or drinks in the kitchen. I love to slice or chop them and add them to eggs or any meat or vegetable dish. Limequat bushes and fruits can exceed those of the parent species in size, and consistently produce more fruit by weight than any other citrus I've grown.

A limequat cluster seen close up.

The flowers have a nice citrus fragrance. Limequats are an easy citrus to grow as bonsai, making a larger specimen from five to eight feet tall. They tolerate temperatures a little below freezing if grown outside as a patio tree in mild climates. Soil should be well drained and allowed to dry out slightly between waterings. Regular watering and fertilizing will contribute to the health and productivity of your limequat bonsai, providing a generous crop to use in the kitchen. Limequats are generally trouble-free and self-pollinating, but they can be susceptible to infestations by scale or mealy bugs, which are best removed with high-pressure sprays or alcohol swabs.

Loquat (*Eriobotrya japonica*) Loquats are a member of the rose family native to China, with a small fruit similar to an apple. The fruits are eaten fresh, canned, and cooked into jams, wines, and desserts. Loquats are very popular and widely grown for their fruits in Asia. They have been introduced all over the world, and there are hundreds, if not thousands, of cultivars with wide variations in fruit shape and color. The fruits are one to two inches in diameter, growing in clusters; they turn yellow when ripe and have a central core of large seeds. The loquat has thick, dark-green

Though this fifty-five-inch loquat has not yet produced fruit in its five years of training, it is a graceful specimen.

leaves up to twelve inches long, with serrated edges and a rusty red hairiness on the underside that provides a striking contrast. The leaves form a whorled pinwheel at the branch tips, creating a unique appearance. The white flowers are quite fragrant, with a sweet smell. I trained a fetching specimen for six years and finally sold it to a client before it ever fruited for me. A loquat is best cultivated as a larger bonsai specimen because of the large leaves, and may need several years of pruning to fill out a crown. There is a variegated loquat grown indoors as an ornamental variety in some areas. Loquats grow slowly, but are drought tolerant and adapt to many different climates and soil types without problems.

Myrtle-leaved orange (*Citrus myrtifolia*) Though it is sometimes described as just a cultivar of *C. auranteum*, which includes other sour oranges like the Seville, the myrtle-leaved orange is different enough to be considered a separate species. With its compact, branching, thornless habit and tiny myrtle-shaped leaves with very short internodes, this is the most dwarf type of citrus I've grown; it has great potential to create a classic bonsai just a couple feet tall. Its small, round fruit have a loose rind and are quite sour, with some bitterness in the peel. When ripe, the fruits will hang for a long time on the tree without going bad, so they can be left to add to the beauty of the bonsai and picked when needed. Introduced to Europe hundreds of years before sweet oranges were discovered, myrtle-leaved oranges have a long history of medicinal and culinary use. The fruits have a strong orange flavor, and are best using in cooking rather than eating fresh. Their high pectin content makes them ideal for use in candy, marmalade, chutneys, and sauces. Myrtle-leaved oranges can be used in all kinds of drinks, and are the source of the orange flavoring agent in classic orange liqueurs.

Clusters of young myrtle-leaved oranges.

Myrtle-leaved oranges need a rich, acidic soil, regular watering, and bright light. This is a slow-growing tree that won't need a huge pot and likely won't need repotting every year. If you wish to create a classic small indoor bonsai with citrus flowers and fruit, the myrtle-leaved orange tree is the best possible candidate.

Natal plum (*Carissa macrocarpa*) Natal (pronounced nuh-**tol**) plum is a dwarf evergreen shrub native to South Africa. It has thick waxy leaves, strong thorns, fragrant white flowers reminiscent of gardenia, and edible red plum-like fruits. A number of varieties are grown as ornamentals in coastal and desert environments, as Natal plum is salt and drought tolerant and very tough. I've seen them come back from being shriveled and wilted. All parts of this plant are poisonous except the tasty fruit, yet it is planted widely as an ornamental in warm climates in the United States. Its dangerous-looking double thorns no doubt contribute to it being advertised as a child- and pet-proof hedge for warm climates. Few people eat the fruit, which is very high in vitamin C and can be used fresh, baked into pastries or other dishes, and made into jams, jellies, or

Top: The thornless variegated dwarf Natal plum bears the same fragrant flowers and tasty fruits as the full sized green variety, but has spectacular foliage. This seventeen-inch specimen has been in training for seven months from a one gallon nursery stock plant.

Bottom: This ripe Natal plum is about an inch and a half long.

sauces. Well known among indoor bonsai enthusiasts, Natal plum can be found at nurseries that carry a good selection of bonsai stock. These plants are well known for creating cascade bonsai where the crown hangs well below the bottom of the pot, as if growing off the edge of a cliff. Natal plums bloom freely with a delightfully scented five-lobed white flower. They bloom most heavily in the spring and summer, but also produce scattered flowers throughout the year, often flowering and fruiting simultaneously. A small plant less than a year old is likely to flower a couple of times a year with bright light; an older medium-to-large specimen with a thick crown can be expected to have flowers open more days than not over a year. There are many cultivated varieties, but the standard, full-sized original plant flowers and fruits much more heavily than any of the dwarf cultivars in my experience. Some dwarfs just have smaller leaves, thorns, flowers, and fruit, and a shorter internode length on the stem; I've trained an attractive golden variegated Natal plum of this type. There are also some extremely compact thornless varieties with an almost otherworldly appearance, including a gorgeous cream and light-green variegated cultivar. That thornless variegated dwarf variety is one of the bestselling bonsai in my nursery, and reliably blooms in two- to three-inch pots in less than a year. These very compact varieties are especially suited for cascades, as they develop dense, heavy crowns on thin trunks and branches. Natal plum will survive a light frost with some damage, but can't really tolerate temperatures below freezing. I have seen them four feet tall with four-inch trunks in landscaping around

This fifty-seven-inch-tall Natal plum has been in training for about eight years, starting as a five-gallon nursery plant. The flowers are very fragrant and the plums are tasty.

hotel pools in Phoenix, Arizona; such plants, if salvaged when slated for removal, would make spectacular bonsai in that climate. There is also a ground-cover variety of Natal plum that resembles a vine with small leaves, flowers, and fruit, and a long distance between leaf nodes. With heavy pruning this can make a very interesting cascade bonsai. The various Natal plums are among my favorite plants for bonsai. The delightfully fragrant flowers and tasty fruit make for an interesting contrast with the wicked thorns and poisonous-looking milky-white latex sap, which seeps out when the fruit is plucked. I often recommend Natal plums to beginners because they are easy to grow and drought-tolerant, and can easily recover if watering is a little late. They do want their water, but should be allowed to dry out between waterings in well-drained potting soil. They can sometimes be infested with scale or mealy bug pests that should be controlled by hand, with alcohol swabs and/or high pressure water sprays. A mature Natal plum bonsai specimen will bloom more consistently than any other species discussed in this book, making it a very desirable species to grow.

New Zealand tea tree (*Leptospermum scoparium*) New Zealand tea tree is often seen in bonsai displays. The tiny sharp leaves and scattered white to pink button-sized flowers on the small bush make it a very attractive plant to train as bonsai. While it has been used to brew tea, this is not the same plant as the tea tree (*Melaleuca* sp.) that produces the widely used tea-tree oil. The wood of the New Zealand tea tree is used for flavoring when smoking meats and fish. Though this plant may not be as useful as others discussed here, its tiny scale and delicate appearance can create a classic small traditional bonsai that flowers freely. While adapted to dry climates, this species can be temperamental if it gets too dry between waterings. I have carved and replanted large five-gallon potted cone-shaped topiaries of New Zealand tea tree to make impressive bonsai in a single afternoon. As part of a collection, the New Zealand tea tree makes a nice contrast to the larger-leaved varieties grown for their fruit.

Papaya (*Carica papaya*) Papaya normally grows as a single-stem trunk, but can be pruned to force branching. Although it will have large leaves, a papaya makes an interesting and attractive bonsai. The best way to start a papaya bonsai is to purchase a fresh papaya at a local market and sprout the seeds by washing and drying them and then planting them right away. Keep them warm and wet, and they will sprout and grow quickly. Whether cultivated as a single trunk or pruned to cause branching, papayas have a striking appearance. I have grown fruit-bearing papayas from seed to a height of five feet in my Colorado home.

Pineapple guava (*Feijoa sellowiana*) Pineapple guava is a larger tree with gray-green textured leaves and flaky tan to rust-colored bark. Older specimens produce spectacular flowers in the form of a large cluster of bright red stamens surrounded by thick, fleshy white petals. These are edible and quite tasty. In the plant's natural habitat in South America, birds often eat the petals, which is believed to facilitate pollination. My older specimens bloom every year but have yet to produce any fruit for me, even with efforts at hand pollination. Some varieties are self-fruiting, while others need cross-pollination to set fruit. While pineapple guavas are easy to grow, they are a bit fussy, needing a cold chilling period to set flower buds. Hot weather and/or lack of pollinators can prevent fruit set. This is an attractive tree that will make a larger-sized bonsai; it's worth growing just for the flowers even if it doesn't fruit. Pineapple guavas need a rich, well-drained soil with plenty of humus, which should be allowed to dry briefly between watering. Due to their relatively open growth habit, they require regular pruning over a

Pineapple guava flower petals are white on the outside and red on the inside, but they curl shortly after opening, hiding the red inside.

The red stamens and curled white petals of these pineapple guava blooms create a strikingly beautiful flower that is also good to eat.

couple years to develop a nice crown. Like some of the other large plant varieties discussed here, pineapple guavas can get overgrown. In this case is possible to dramatically prune the specimen, removing as much as seventy-five percent of the tree, while leaving good-sized woody stumps on major branches. Regular pinching of the resulting shoots will create tight crowns, making for a very dramatic bonsai.

Pineapple sage (*Salvia elegans*) Pineapple sage is a fast-growing woody herb that can become a medium-sized shrub. Growing strongly upright, with square stems that get quite woody, it has large, hairy, pale-green leaves that release a delightful pineapple fragrance when brushed. When I see this plant growing anywhere, even in a garden shop herb display, I can't resist bruising a leaf to smell the fragrance. Its tubular bright-red flowers, which are very attractive to humming-birds and butterflies, arise out of long spikes in the fall, and can bloom throughout the winter indoors. Native to Mexico and Central America, pineapple sage has a long history of medicinal use to relieve anxiety, which is not surprising, as even the scent has a soothing effect. The flowers can be used in teas and salads, and the leaves are made into both hot and cold beverages. They can also be chopped and added to salads or cooked with fruits, vegetables and meats. Try garnishing a cocktail with a sprig of pineapple sage that tickles the nostrils as you sip. While very fast growing, this sage is a woody herb rather than a small tree, and will benefit from a severe pruning every year, perhaps with a root pruning to keep the pot size manageable when providing fresh soil. A good-sized specimen reaching three to four feet in height, with a couple more feet of flowering spikes in season, will produce a fair quantity of leaves and some flowers for culinary use. Use a rich, well-drained soil and a pot a little on the large side, as pineapple sage grows fast. It will need a lot of water when growing actively. A small plant from the herb section of your local garden store can be field-grown or kept in a large pot for a summer. If given plenty of water and fertilizer, it will form a bush that can be cut back and shaped into a very respectable bonsai by the time it is a year old. Pineapple sage will take full sun in the garden and needs good bright light indoors, but is well worth growing.

Rosemary (*Rosmarinus officinalis*) Rosemary is the classic herb most often used for bonsai. The rosemary specimen on the back cover of my 1996 book *Herbal Bonsai* is currently blooming in my greenhouse, mid-fall sixteen years later. I've seen fifty-year-old rosemary trees with four-inch-diameter trunks. With a rich fragrance sometimes described as "piney" and sharp, needle-like leaves, rosemary bonsai resemble classic pines in appearance, but don't require the lifetime of slow, painstaking training. Rosemary has many culinary and medicinal uses. I use

This thirty-six-inch-tall rosemary specimen has been in training for eighteen years. This same tree was displayed in my book 1995 **Herbal Bonsai,** *although it was a double-trunked specimen back then.*

These are flowers from the same rosemary.

homemade rosemary wine in cooking, and a favorite home remedy if I feel like I'm coming down with a bug is to sit in the hot tub with a cup of strong, hot rosemary tea with honey and lemon. Rosemary twigs can soaked in water and thrown on hot coals when grilling. While rosemary should be allowed to dry out between watering, it can get too dry and die suddenly. It grows more rapidly than woody trees and can quickly become root-bound, even in a larger pot, which predisposes it to dry out rapidly. People who suddenly lose the rosemary they are trying to overwinter often have a root-bound specimen in a dry environment, and have allowed it to get a little too dry. Rosemary should be repotted and root-pruned every year, with a corresponding strong crown trim for balance. A small rosemary plant purchased in the spring can be field-grown over a summer growing season and carved into a very nice bonsai specimen in the fall. As rosemary is difficult and slow to grow from seed, it is better to start with a small plant; rosemary cuttings root easily. There are a number of named cultivars, including some with pink or white flowers rather than the typical blue. There is a prostrate version that naturally grows with branches that twist and curve in all directions. While this variety can be used to create cascade bonsai, when pruned in a manner forcing it to grow more upright, older prostrate rosemary shows spectacular character and is far more interesting and beautiful than the standard upright varieties. Rosemary definitely needs lots of bright light to winter indoors, and since that hot direct light will dry out a root-bound plant, watering should be monitored closely.

Sage (*Salvia officinalis*) Common culinary sage, a woody herb with gray-green foliage and blue or purple flowers, can also be grown as a bonsai. Cooks often use this strongly flavored herb, fresh or dried, to season poultry and other meats. It also makes a refreshing tea. One medium-sized sage bonsai will provide all the sage a family might need over a year. Like other herbs, sage will grow fast enough to create a specimen from a small plant in just one year, which is a very short timeframe compared to traditional outdoor bonsai. A mature specimen will require severe pruning (including roots) and repotting every year. There are a number of cultivars with variations in flowers or foliage, including a miniature-leaved variety. There are also striking golden- and purple-leafed varieties and a number of variegated cultivars with shades of white, yellow, green, and purple mixed together in different combinations. These variegated types usually have more tender leaves than the common green sage and are better suited for growing indoors; they also make more attractive bonsai. Sage grown indoors needs very bright light and well-drained potting soil, which should be allowed to dry between waterings, but not for too long.

Savory (*Satureja* sp.) Summer savory (*S. hortensis*) and winter savory (*S. montana*) have fallen out of use these days, despite their long culinary history as a seasoning for beans and meats. The savories have a strong flavor and are used much like sage, whether fresh or dried. Summer savory, considered to have a sweeter flavor, is generally preferred for culinary use. It is also a component of *herbes de Provence*, an herb blend that is a staple of French cooking. The fast-growing summer savory is generally considered an annual, but will get quite woody if cut back repeatedly; it can live for a year or two in warm temperatures and good conditions. To my mind, thisi is just a bonsai on a different timescale. Winter savory is a woody dwarf evergreen shrub with tiny leaves and a compact habit that is well suited to growing as bonsai. Hardy to temperatures well below freezing, it is longer lived than summer savory, and, like traditional outdoor bonsai, will respond well to a colder dormant period. Both species will create small bonsai best suited to limited space or as part of a collection. Both are fairly easy to grow with well-drained potting soil and bright light. Summer savory grows much faster and can provide more harvest than the winter variety, but requires warmer temperatures and frequent pruning to keep it healthy and looking good.

Scented geranium (*Pelargonium* sp.) Scented geraniums comprise a large group with hundreds of widely available named cultivars. Throughout the history of naming plants in this genus, there have been several reclassifications, resulting in much confusion, at least a dozen different species, and numerous cross-hybrids. In my experiences growing more than thirty different cultivars, I've often seen a scented geranium throw off a "sport" that looks totally different from the rest of the plant. Variegated cultivars in particular often sprout a branch with dramatically different variegation, or none at all. Often grown as annuals in temperate climates, scented geraniums are tender perennials that can grow into woody shrubs. There is a wide variety in growth habits, from dwarf trailing bushes to strongly upright dwarf shrubs. The leaves, which often resemble oak leaves, can be tiny or very large, and take shapes ranging from round to finely divided. Leaves range from gray to a clear bright green, and can be all one color, show dark zonal areas, or display bright white, cream, or yellow variegation. Some cultivars have smooth shiny leaves; others can vary from rough to hairy or velvety, looking as if they were cut from crinkled paper. The flowers vary in size, and flower clusters can range from just a few isolated flowers to compact heads with dozens of florets in multiple colors such as white, pink, lavender, red, and yellow, with all shades in between. The distinguishing feature in this group, of course, is the wide variety of fragrances to be found, and this is the reason they are cultivated so widely and with such passion. From fruity scents like apple, apricot, gooseberry, lemon, lime, orange, and strawberry, to spicy ones like ginger, nutmeg, camphor, and cinnamon, to oddities like coconut and chocolate, as well as perhaps the largest group, the various rose fragrances, there is no other closely related group of plants with such a wide range of fragrant foliage. Scented geraniums have a long history of medicinal use in their native Africa, and are widely used in potpourris and tea. The leaves have been used to flavor jellies, butters, sauces, ice cream, and all manner of drinks. The flowers are good in salads and make a fine edible garnish, but most geranium leaves are too tough and fibrous to use raw for consumption. Scented geraniums became very popular in Victorian times, when they were used as "strewing herbs" to cover up bad odors and added to fingerbowls presented to guests between meal courses for rinsing their fingers. Scented geraniums are as easy to cultivate as common geraniums; they grow quickly and will produce an abundance of foliage. Older plants can get quite leggy, needing a severe pruning at least once and possibly several times a year. They will also need repotting and root pruning every year, always accompanied by a sharp top pruning. A geranium confined to a small pot will require this treatment more often. Sometimes a large number of leaves on the interior of a large-crowned specimen will turn yellow and then dry brown. This is an indication that the plant is not getting enough water, and may be a sign that your bonsai is in need of a severe pruning and possibly repotting. These dying leaves can easily be removed by combing the fingers through the branches if you are not ready for such drastic steps right away. Bright light, good potting soil, and regular watering will keep your scented geranium bonsai happy without much specialized care. Try to place it somewhere you can brush it to release the fragrant oils as you walk by, so you can enjoy the aromatherapy every day. My favorite variety is a variegated lemon crispum with bright yellow foliage, small leaves, and pretty patterned flowers, but most small-leafed cultivars work well for bonsai. Even the popular chocolate cultivar with large, velvety maple-like leaves, which grows like a vine rather than upright, gets quite woody and can make a beautiful cascade bonsai growing out of a hanging basket.

Strawberry guava (*Psidium cattleianum*) Some authorities consider this to be a variety of the same species as lemon guava (*P. littorale*). The dark-red fruit of the strawberry guava is smaller and more oblong in shape than the lemon guava, and is sweeter and milder. In my experience, the strawberry guava also bears more heavily: the crop I get every year in late summer is large enough to eat some fresh and ferment the rest into wine. Strawberry guavas ripen over a one- to two-month period, needing to be picked every couple of days, so I freeze any I don't eat fresh. One can enjoy a regular fresh harvest over a relatively long season for a soft fruit, or save them to make jelly or wine that can be savored all year long. It is easy to understand the naming confusion, as strawberry guava and lemon guava plants look so much alike that it's very difficult to tell them apart unless they are fruiting. A fast-growing bush with attractive cinnamon-colored bark that peels away from its light-colored underbark, the strawberry guava makes a larger bonsai, and may need severe pruning at times to keep it at a manageable size. I haven't had any pest problems with this plant, but in tropical areas where they have been widely introduced and are sometimes considered an invasive species, the fruits are subject to heavy fruit-fly infestation before ripening, which makes them inedible. If you have the space to grow this as a larger specimen, it is a beautiful tree that

Ripe strawberry guava.

This strawberry guava was pruned down to sixty-seven inches after being dug out of the ground in the greenhouse. Four months later, it was seventy-six inches tall, as shown here.

Flower clusters on a strawberry tree.

can bear a heavy crop of tasty fruit. Every summer, I give visitors to my Colorado greenhouse the chance to taste fresh-picked guavas from my six large lemon- and strawberry-guava bonsais.

Strawberry tree (*Arbutus unedo*) The strawberry tree is an ornamental evergreen native to the Mediterranean region, with dark glossy oval leaves that have finely toothed edges. It is often planted ornamentally as a hedge in suitable climates. In fall, it bears clusters of small white bell-shaped flowers that develop into round strawberry-like fruits no larger than an inch in diameter; a strawberry-tree bonsai may have flowers and fruit simultaneously. While not exactly juicy and delectable, the fruits can be used to make jams and flavor drinks. The tree's peeling, rust-colored bark makes a striking contrast to its shiny green leaves. The strawberry tree can send out shoots or suckers from low on the trunk; these should be removed to keep a single-trunk bonsai shape. While considered a slow grower, a strawberry tree can reach twenty feet or more planted in the ground. It will tolerate periods of below-freezing temperatures, although this may prevent fruiting. Its size and cold tolerance make the strawberry tree a good candidate for a patio bonsai in places that don't get too cold. The strawberry tree has a long history, and has appeared in writing and works of art as far back as the Roman era. This history, as well as its unique fruit, make it a very interesting plant to grow. It requires well-drained soil, which should be kept on the dry side, and needs very bright light indoors.

Sweet marjoram (*Origanum majorana*) Sweeter than its cousin oregano, yet with a stronger scent, sweet marjoram is another herb native to the Mediterranean that has become a staple in kitchens everywhere. This small, tender perennial shrub seldom grows more than a foot tall, and has soft gray-green foliage and tiny white flowers. Left on its own, sweet marjoram will grow as a multi-stemmed bush, but can be trained into a beautiful miniature bonsai. The strong shoots that may sprout out of the ground or from the trunk and roots should be removed unless a multi-trunk bonsai is desired; in this case, it could even be replanted deeper to create a "forest grove" from several shoots. These shoots can be used fresh or dried and saved for many uses in the kitchen. Marjoram can be substituted for oregano, blends well with nearly any other herb, and makes a delightful relaxing tea. Though it is usually grown as an annual, sweet marjoram can live for years; it is another herb that can be made into a "mature" bonsai in one summer growing season, starting with a small garden-shop plant purchased in the spring. Sweet marjoram can survive a light frost, but is sensitive to freezing temperatures. It does well in a bright window indoors, though it may get a little leggy if light is not optimal. This is easily managed by continuously trimming the plant and using the harvest. Your sweet marjoram bonsai will thrive in rich but well-drained soil with regular watering and occasional doses of fertilizer.

Sweet myrtle (*Myrtus communis* var. *Compacta*) This miniature-leaved myrtle is a cultivar of the common myrtle, which has been revered through history and mentioned in the Bible and many early Greek and Roman texts. Numerous cultures have incorporated myrtle in their rituals and traditions. The plant was considered to be sacred to the goddesses Aphrodite and Venus, symbolic of love and immortality. Because of this, myrtle branches are still commonly used as greenery in floral shops, especially in bouquets and arrangements for weddings. The leaves, flowers, and fruit of the sweet myrtle are edible, having a strong flavor. The white flowers are star-shaped, with five petals and an intense yet pleasant fragrance. The dark-green leaves are small, sharp, and tough. When used as a seasoning with meats or stews, the leaves should be left on their branches and removed after cooking rather than being consumed directly. The sweet berries are used to flavor traditional Greek liqueurs, sometimes with the leaves added. Try infusing a clear spirit like vodka with the dark-purple berries to create your own sweet myrtle liqueur; it can be served over ice or as part of a cocktail, perhaps with a sprig of myrtle as a garnish. Dwarf sweet myrtle can be found in the bonsai, topiary, and herb sections of most garden centers, and is sometimes available as larger plants in one-, two-, or five-gallon nursery pots that can be carved into an impressive bonsai in a few hours. The standard common myrtle can also be trained into a larger bonsai specimen. There is an attractive yellow variegated cultivar used in topiaries that makes a beautiful bonsai with bright foliage. One of my favorite cultivars is twisted myrtle (*M. communis* var. *boetica*), a larger specimen with similar flavors and fragrance to sweet myrtle, but with long leaves that whorl around the stem and point sharply upright. As it is more resistant to drought and cold than other cultivars, twisted myrtle is becoming widely available in places like the southwestern US, where it is used for landscaping. From a distance, a twisted myrtle bonsai specimen can resemble a candelabrum, with individual branches looking like inch-thick green candles. Its unique appearance always attracted attention in my bonsai displays. Sweet myrtle is fairly easy to grow with bright light, well-drained soil, and plenty of water when needed. Scale and mealy bug can be attracted to myrtles, and should be controlled by hand, water sprays, and soap rather than poisonous insecticides. Be careful to look for pests when purchasing myrtles, especially in nurseries where large groups are grown outside. In the back lots and remote greenhouses of plant stores in places like Phoenix, where many myrtles are grown and used for landscaping, it is possible to find an old neglected specimen with incredible character that can be carved back into a very impressive bonsai. The long history and culture associated with sweet myrtle is enough to make the plant a very interesting and desirable addition to your edible indoor bonsai garden.

Thyme (*Thymus* sp.) Common or English thyme (*T. vulgaris*) is the widely used culinary variety of thyme, but the genus contains more than 300 species, both scented and unscented. Thyme is widely used for landscaping, can tolerate subfreezing temperatures, but may also be grown indoors. So many species and cultivars are used in the commercial markets that there is much confusing overlap in common names; there are dozens of different varieties called "creeping thyme." There are also numerous lemon-scented thymes (*T. citriodorus*), including both upright bushes and creeping groundcovers, the most popular of which is Aureus, a gorgeous golden variegated cultivar with an upright growth habit. There is also a white variegated cultivar, as well as others that smell of orange or lime. Caraway thyme (*T. herba-barona*) is a tiny-leaved plant with dark-green leaves and a strong caraway fragrance that is usually considered a groundcover. I once purchased a one-gallon nursery plant of this species, exposed several inches of buried trunk, and removed two-thirds of the crown to create a spectacular six-inch-tall bonsai with a compact crown and a half-inch diameter trunk. My favorite thyme for bonsai is conehead thyme (*T. capitatus*), a cultivar I came across at a nursery in Tucson, Arizona. It has very fine gray-green foliage and develops a very thick trunk for its size, with splintery gray bark. It gets its name from the compact flower heads that develop on the branch tips, which actually resemble little pinecones with little white flowers that erupt around the cone. Many cultivars of creeping thyme (*T. serpyllum*) are used in landscaping; the color of their flowers and foliage varies, as does their fragrance. Though these may not be suitable for shaping as bonsai themselves, they can make very attractive groundcover accent plants around the base of larger bonsai. I'll sometimes visit a garden center before a bonsai show to pick up a small, inexpensive creeping thyme to tuck into the pot of a particular bonsai specimen. One of my favorite varieties for this is woolly thyme (*T. pseudolanuginosus*), which is less than an inch tall with tiny, fuzzy, gray foliage. Most varieties of thyme will tolerate some freezing temperatures in landscaping, but when trained as bonsai they should be kept indoors, where they will do well. Thyme can tolerate some dryness; it needs well-drained soil and very bright light. New shoots may sprout from anywhere on the plant, making it quite bushy and thick if not pruned regularly. Save all your trimmings when shaping a thyme bonsai. Besides its culinary uses, thyme contains thymol, an antiseptic and antifungal essential oil that is an active ingredient in many over-the-counter preparations, from mouthwashes to hand sanitizers. I've made thyme wines and jellies to use in cooking. Thyme keeps its flavor well when dried, and a little goes a long way in cooking. With its tiny leaves and compact shape, thyme can make a spectacular classic bonsai in a small size. Keeping it perfectly trimmed may require more detailed work than most other edible bonsai, but it is well worth the effort.

CHAPTER 4

Finding Your Future Bonsai

T he best place to find any of the plants discussed in this book is at your local garden center or plant shop. In my twenty years of operating a wholesale tropical bonsai business, I've visited hundreds of garden centers in more than two dozen states, selling them bonsai and staying on the lookout for potential new species to train as bonsai. Many of the plants in my collection were acquired this way. While nurseries generally sell many of the same varieties, their plant buyers all have personal preferences and interests that influence their plant selections. Explore as many garden centers as you can, and visit them when you travel, because different regions have their own selections and local suppliers who may grow something unique that is not distributed widely.

It should be noted that efforts to control the spread of plant diseases have resulted in an increasing number of restrictions and laws governing the movement of plants between states. These have had a severe effect on horticultural enterprises in some regions. In Texas, for example, only citrus plants propagated within the state may be sold; citrus cannot be imported into the state for resale. Many southern and western states are beginning to enact similar laws. Because most of the plants discussed here are grown and used in landscaping in these milder climates, however, they are readily available locally in those states. There is no need to bring a citrus tree from Iowa to Texas, but there would be no restrictions on purchasing a tree in Texas to take back to Iowa. Be sure to check your state agricultural laws if you plan to bring plants across state lines.

Keeping those restrictions in mind, searching garden centers when traveling to milder climates is the best way to find a wide selection of the largely tropical plants best suited for indoor edible bonsai. An edible fig tree can usually be obtained anywhere in the continental US by visiting a large garden center or two, especially one near a large metropolitan area. Even a store in a colder climate might have half a dozen specimens of one or possibly two varieties. When visiting a bonsai client of mine, a medium-sized garden center in Austin, Texas, where figs can survive when planted in the landscape, I found fifteen different varieties of edible fig with over a hundred plants to choose from in the fruit section of their nursery. A couple of them came home with me to Colorado. Natal plums are widely available; the best specimen in my collection came from a group of old five-gallon nursery plants in the corner of a neglected greenhouse outside Phoenix, Arizona, that had rooted through the pots well into the ground. I yanked out eight of them to take home. One died from the shock, and I kept one for myself, but the rest made a spectacular group of specimens that my bonsai business sold very quickly. I found Chilean guavas as good-sized nursery stock in Portland, Oregon, which has a mild enough climate for them to survive. Visiting local nurseries in places like this is clearly the best way to find a large variety of suitable plants for edible bonsai, with enough selection to choose the best potential specimen from a group of plants. Not everyone is in a position to drive somewhere to find and bring plants back, however. If you have traveled to a warmer location by air, you can package your selected specimen to ship via one of the large retail shipping companies. If the plant is well watered and is kept at temperatures above freezing, it will survive an inexpensive five-day ground shipment quite well.

Visiting a nursery in person lets you look at the plants and see exactly what you are getting. Individual specimens in any group of plants of the same pot size and species will vary greatly. Besides checking for pests and overall health of the plant, a discerning eye can pick out one or two plants in the group with the potential to create spectacular bonsai. Having a good selection of plants to sort through is especially important when creating an "instant" bonsai from a larger plant. Because you cannot control the shape from the very beginning, as you can with a small plant, you must be able to work with what the plant gives you from its previous growth. It is always a good idea to develop a relationship with a large, well-stocked garden shop where you will have a good selection of plants and can get expert advice if you have any problems. Get to know the tropical plant person or greenhouse manager at that shop. They want to carry what you wish to buy, so if you want something unusual and can't find it, ask for it. They are likely to have a source for it, and may even decide to begin selling an interesting plant you request.

Some of the varieties discussed in this book are becoming prevalent as indoor bonsai specimens, and can be found at any plant shop that carries a good selection of bonsai plants and supplies. Dwarf pomegranates, Natal plums, and Australian cherries are often sold as already trained bonsai specimens; many nurseries also offer them as "bonsai starters" in four- or six-inch pots. The commonly sold one-, two-, or five-gallon nursery stock plants of these three species can be used to create an attractive bonsai specimen in a few hours. Many herbs and scented geraniums can be found at garden centers with an herb department. These plants grow very quickly from an inexpensive three- to four-inch plant. By pushing their growth over a summer growing season, it is possible to create a "mature" bonsai specimen in less than a year, while also learning more about shaping a bonsai than you would in years of working with slow-growing traditional bonsai plants like junipers and pines. Some of these herbs and scented geraniums can be found in one-gallon nursery pots, which will give you a head start on growing your bonsai. Rosemary is so popular as a landscape

The branches of this twenty-eight-inch-tall green calamondin orange are bent almost into a circle by the weight of its fruit.

feature that it can be found at many nurseries in even larger pots up to five gallons in size. A large nursery plant like this can create a spectacular herbal bonsai in a couple hours. Many of these herbs and geraniums, as well as some of the myrtles, can also be found at plant shops as topiaries. Those may or may not have the perfect shape to train as bonsai, but will give you something to start with.

Most large well-stocked nurseries, even in cold northern climates, carry a selection of citrus. Oranges, grapefruit, lemons, and limes are widely available, but not all nurseries have the more unusual smaller citrus that in my experience are easier to grow and bear far more fruit indoors in cold climates. Calamondin oranges, my favorite citrus to use in cooking, are the easiest small citrus to find in local nurseries. I usually recommend calamondins to first-time citrus growers because they are the easiest citrus to grow indoors and can bear ripe fruit for long periods during the year, usually producing two crops annually. Kumquats and Key limes can be found in many places, although limequats, Buddha's hand citron, myrtle-leaved orange, and other unusual citrus are not as common.

Hibiscus can be found everywhere, although you might need to search harder for miniature varieties. Hot peppers can be started from seed or purchased at garden shops everywhere in the spring. Ornamental peppers are widely available and can often be found in garden shops as plants that are large and woody enough to create a nice bonsai in a very short time. Coffee

Strawberry tree as purchased from a local nursery.

Myrtle-leaved orange tree as purchased from a local nursery.

trees can be found at nearly any plant store that brings in four-inch foliage plant selections out of Florida. Figs, jasmines, and olives can be found in nurseries in most areas, although you may have to visit a few different shops. The more unusual tropical fruits can be difficult to find, but they are out there. My wholesale bonsai business has sold most of the varieties in this book as bonsai specimens across much of the United States. There are good, innovative greenhouse managers out there, even in far northern climates, who bring in a large variety of tropical specimens—not only citrus, but also guavas, mangos, bananas, dragon fruit, and other exotics, providing new horizons to explore in creating edible bonsai. The plants used to illustrate Chapter 2, "Creating Instant Bonsai," were purchased from a retail nursery in Fort Collins, Colorado, less than twenty miles from my home.

Key lime tree as purchased from a local nursery.

In this day and age, of course, nearly anything can be found on the Internet. Type a plant name into a search engine, and several places to purchase it will probably pop up. Prices may be high, even before shipping, and they will most likely be small plants for you to train rather than mature specimens, but even small plants just shipped can bear fruit. Online ordering can be a good option for someone who can't travel to numerous garden stores or who is looking for a hard-to-find specimen. I found my green tea bushes in an online advertisement from a company that was actually marketing the plants as novelty items to coffee and tea shops, rather than to nurseries and plant shops. They were small, spindly plants in four-inch pots, and I now propagate new plants by taking cuttings from that original shipment I received. Learning to root cuttings using rooting hormones is a great way both to acquire new plants and to multiply your own specimens from the trimmings of an existing bonsai. I have acquired new species by rooting a gift cutting from someone with a unique specimen.

Rescuing plants from an outdoor garden that is about to be torn up or frozen in the fall is another good way to obtain plants, and doesn't cost anything. Sometimes spectacular specimens can be created from mature plants out of old gardens. At one time I lived near the national headquarters of a large insurance compa-

This six-inch Barbados cherry had ripe fruit just weeks after being shipped to me by a wholesale bonsai grower as a starter bonsai in a 4 inch plastic pot.

ny that maintained a free public garden on their grounds. One feature was a circular raised bed that was planted as a scent garden with annual and perennial fragrant plants. After years of taking friends to visit, I realized they left the annuals to die at the first freeze in the fall and replanted every spring. One summer they had a unique group of scented geraniums, including one that I lusted after—a tiny-leaved cream-and-green variegated cultivar called Gooseberry, which had a delightful fruity scent. One fall night, during a snowstorm that was leading into the first hard freeze that year, I went to that garden and dug several scented geraniums out of the ground. I was uneasy about doing this, but the plants would have died that night anyway. I felt like a plant superhero, flouting society's conventions to rescue victims from certain death. I then propagated the plants and spread them around for others to enjoy. I admit to being obsessive about collecting specimens for use as bonsai, especially if I can use or eat part of the plant. If you keep your eyes open and stay observant, there are potential candidates for edible bonsai everywhere.

Let's say that when it comes time for you to pick out your plant for bonsai, you're at a garden shop with a broad selection of plants to choose from. You must examine these candidates closely. The first step is to evaluate their overall health and appearance and check for insect pests. Bugs can be hard to see, so look closely under the leaves and at the tender growing shoots where they are likely to gather. Once this is done, the most important characteristic to check is the size and shape of the trunk and main branches of your potential bonsai. Though some of those branches can be pruned, you must choose a plant with a basic shape and arrangement of branches you can work with. Some plants may only need minor pruning to look good, but many will need half or more of the branches and foliage removed to begin shaping as bonsai. Try to find the inner bonsai within the plant. Look for a nice, thick trunk with major branches that are arranged in such a way as to give a good shape to what will be the base or skeleton of your bonsai. Pop the plant out of its pot to examine the roots. Showing off the base of the trunk and large, exposed roots will add greatly to the character and apparent age of the bonsai. Root systems can vary a lot, depending on the species and how long the plant has been in the pot. Nurseries often plant a plug or small plant deeply into a nursery pot, and because roots grow down, not up, as a rule, the top inch or two of soil can be removed with little root damage, exposing more trunk and interestingly shaped roots. Australian cherries, in particular, can reveal large, elaborately twisted roots. One last consideration is the presence of flowers or fruit on the plant. While this can be very desirable, and helps create a spectacular specimen overnight, keep in mind that the branches that the fruit or flowers are on may need to be removed to shape the bon-sai. Furthermore, repotting your plant to fit into a bonsai pot, especially if severe root pruning is involved, can cause plants to drop any remaining fruit. If the fruit harvest is important, sometimes a small branch with fruit can be left on the bonsai until after the fruit is picked. It is quite possible to create a spectacular "instant" bonsai from a flowering or fruiting plant. I've done this type of carving thousands of times to make bonsai for my wholesale business. It can be very rewarding to create a beautiful minia-ture orange bonsai with flowers and ripe fruit in an afternoon's work.

CHAPTER 5

Long-Term Bonsai Care

Many people, on seeing pictures of beautiful traditional bonsai displayed in Japanese homes, have tried to do the same thing, only to have their juniper die quickly. They don't realize that the bonsai they saw was grown and maintained in a suitable outdoor environment. Traditional bonsai are only brought in from the garden to display in the house for a couple of days; they are then moved back to the proper environment, with a different specimen then rotated in for display. All plants need suitable conditions to thrive, and unfortunately, when someone picks a place to display a bonsai in the home, it isn't necessarily the best place for that plant to grow. There are a number of ways to deal with this problem. Obviously, the traditional practice of maintaining a collection in a suitable place and rotating specimens into the home for short periods is ideal. Because most of the varieties in this book are from tropical or Mediterranean climates and won't tolerate much in the way of freezing temperatures, this would require a greenhouse or a good-sized solar room, at least during the coldest months, unless you live in a very mild climate. Many readers, however, will be looking to create specimens that will fit in a permanent location in the home. This book also focuses on creating larger bonsai, partly because crop production is a priority, and partly because some of these desirable species are large-leaved plants which need that size to look good. A six-foot bonsai in a twenty-four-inch pot is not easy to rotate in and out of the house every couple of days. Instead, it is preferable to create the proper environment for your bonsai within your home.

When it comes to an indoor setting, the most critical condition is lighting. All of the plants discussed here need bright light to thrive and bear a harvest. Again, a greenhouse or solar room is obviously the best environment, but most people don't have those kinds of spaces available. Light from east, south, and west windows should suffice to keep bonsai alive, but they need to be right in the window. The heat of direct sun can dry out plants quickly, so paying close attention to the watering schedule is a must. West windows are usually brighter and hotter than east ones, and south windows are best in winter, especially in northern areas where days are shorter and the sun is lower in the sky. Even in the brightest window, your bonsai will turn its leaves toward the window to absorb the sunlight, and new growth will be in that direction as well. Because of this, bonsai should be rotated regularly, every week or so, to keep them balanced.

Most indoor bonsai benefit from spending time outdoors when the weather is suitable. Because of the greater amount of light and wind, bonsai tend to dry out faster outside, and will need more frequent watering. Sunburn is also an important consideration. Indoor windows will block the UV rays that cause sunburn, but a bonsai moved from an indoor location to full bright sun outside is likely to get sunburned. This effect is amplified at higher altitudes where the sun is more intense. At my 6,000-foot altitude in Colorado I have had even sun-loving citrus burn after a couple of days in full sun. Bonsai can usually recover from sunburn, but the sunburned foliage will be ruined. Be sure to place your bonsai where it will be shaded during the middle of the day when the sun is overhead and at its most intense.

Not everyone has an ideal window for fruiting bonsai, and the most sun-loving plants discussed here, like citrus and most herbs, will stretch and grow toward the light in even the best window. Depending on your situation, you may want to add some artificial lighting. For most situations, adding a little extra light to a less-than-ideal window is good option for keeping your bonsai happy. Long-tube fluorescent plant lights are easy to find, but they are are unattractive and don't really work well anyway, as they are only intense enough to provide adequate light a few inches from the bulb. This makes them ideal for growing seedlings, but not so effective for an odd-shaped bonsai that is several feet tall. There are large thousand-watt commercial plant lights that can be hung high and will illuminate a room-sized area, but they are expensive, burn lots of energy, and are not suitable for a living area (a light like this could, however, be used to illuminate a growing space for a collection, even where there is no natural sunlight). A better choice is a small incandescent spotlight-type full-spectrum plant bulb. These range from 75 to 150 watts, do put out some heat, and are designed to operate at a distance of four to ten feet from the plant. They screw into regular light-bulb sockets, so they can fit into lamps that are suitable for a living space, and are inexpensive and easily available at any store that has a large light-bulb selection. This is an ideal solution to add extra light and balance the unidirectional light from a window. A 150-watt bulb can illuminate an area a yard square, giving enough light to grow a small specimen even in the absence of natural light. I would recommend using a timer to keep the lighting consistent. A bonsai in an east-facing window will benefit from extra light later in the day; one in a west window needs the extra light earlier in the day. You can also turn the lights on in the evening during short winter days to help you enjoy viewing your bonsai. Many plants are quite sensitive to day length and can be stimulated to flower out of their normal season with increased—or, in some cases, decreased—day length.

Potting soils are not as critical as light conditions, and a good indoor houseplant potting soil will generally work well. Extra peat moss can be added for plants like citrus or green tea, which prefer a more acid soil. The soil can also be amended with acid fertilizers. Extra organic matter or vermiculite can be added for plants like Australian cherries or figs, which use lots of water and benefit from soil that holds more moisture. Garden centers also carry "water crystals" under various trade names, which are polymer crystals that absorb forty times their weight in water. Small quantities mixed into potting soil will absorb extra water and release it as the soil dries out. These can be very beneficial for bonsai that need constant moisture or are restricted to smaller pots that dry out quickly. For plants that need well-drained soil, such as herbs and many tree species, perlite, coarse building sand, or very small rock chips can be added to the same basic houseplant potting soil to improve drainage. Most of these plants are not extremely fussy, and with careful watering will survive in nearly any good potting soil, even without additional amendments.

This book departs significantly from bonsai tradition by using bigger and deeper pots than are conventionally used. By traditional standards, the ideal bonsai pot is no deeper than the diameter of the trunk of the tree it holds. This is possible with slow-growing traditional outdoor bonsai that have been in training for many years, though very careful watering is required to keep the specimen alive. Most of the varieties we are using for edible bonsai are active year-round, and grow faster than most traditional bonsai. They need more room for their roots, and using bigger pots makes it much easier to keep them alive. Precise watering is less critical and you won't have to repot as often. These species require more frequent repotting than slow-growing bonsai that go through a dormant season. Herbs and geraniums in particular will become root-bound in less than a year no matter what size pot you use, and will benefit from an annual severe pruning, including the roots. Depending on the plant's growth and how much it is pruned back, your bonsai may fit back into the same pot, but will usually do better if moved up to a slightly bigger pot. It is critical to give it fresh soil and room to grow. Slower-growing shrubs and trees can go a couple of years between repottings, and need them less frequently as they age. Always prune the crown when repotting a bonsai to balance the water loss through leaf transpiration with the reduced water uptake through the disturbed and pruned roots.

Edible fig trees in particular need big pots. Figs have large, aggressive root systems that can reach quite a distance when searching for water. Although they are known for thriving in dry climates and can tolerate drought when dormant, they need lots of water when leafed out and producing fruit. Use as big a pot as you can and water heavily when the plant is fruiting. In my opinion, with bright light, good soil drainage, and a crown full of leaves and fruit, it is impossible to overwater a fig tree.

Using bigger pots than is traditional will benefit all of these edible bonsai and make it easier for you to keep them thriving; however, it means the pot will have a more prominent place in your artistic presentation. The appearance of the larger soil surface can make a big difference in how your edible bonsai looks. Because traditional mosses won't survive in a dry indoor environment, my basic solution is to cover the soil with a fine gravel or coarse sand. Coarser gravel can be used on larger specimens. A local sand, gravel, and rock company can offer a wide selection and will likely let you get a bucket or two of gravel at minimal cost. An attractive, well-placed rock can provide the perfect accent to a bonsai specimen while decorating the expansive surface. With a big surface, an arrangement of rocks—always using an odd number and random-seeming placement—can bring to mind a natural scene, as if one were walking through the hills and spotted this beautiful aged tree. With larger pots it is also possible to use an accent plant like baby tears (*Soleirolia* or *Helxine soleirolii*), although this common greenhouse plant must be kept wet, and may not work with plants that need to dry out between watering. A better choice for most plants would be a dwarf, low-growing compact sedum (*Sedum* sp.) or one of the creeping thymes (*T. serpyllum* or *T. pseudolanuginosus*). Irish moss (*Sagina subulata*) or the golden "Aurea" Scottish moss, with its tiny attractive white flowers, also make a stunning appearance with very tiny scale. These plants can fill the ground over a year, and may need to be pulled out and divided before the bonsai needs repotting.

In addition, bonsai shops usually carry selection of "mud men"—small figurines of people, animals, or buildings that are often used to decorate bonsai.

These dwarf Australian cherries planted in a forest grove setting are full of flower buds. This specimen is twenty-six inches tall.

While I prefer a more natural look, everyone has different preferences, and if you like the idea you should decorate your edible bonsai with whatever suits your fancy. I once placed a small round mirror with hidden edges on a bonsai and it looked just like a small pond, needing only a small "mud men" boat to complete the illusion. Your bonsai is an artistic creation, and you should carry out your theme and vision through the groundcover.

Another way to display bonsai is to combine several trees into a forest or grove planting. All trees in a grove should be of the same variety, and they should be odd in number. Australian cherries work well like this. I have always wanted an orange grove, and bonsai allow me to have one, even in Colorado.

Traditional bonsai authorities advise using fertilizers only sparingly, as slow-growing outdoor trees that should be only a foot or two tall when they are a hundred years old or more will not look good if growth is pushed. Traditional bonsai are fertilized very lightly just once a year in early spring; fertilizing later in the summer can push late soft growth that may not survive through a cold dormant season. Most bonsai guides advise using fertilizers at half strength, and some recommend using a mild organic fish emulsion as a gentle fertilizer. Edible bonsai, on the other hand, should be fertilized regularly, just like any other houseplant. As most of the species best suited for edible bonsai are from tropical or Mediterranean climates, they don't go dormant and can grow all year. They are also faster-growing species that need to be fed more often; the time and size scale is very different from that of traditional bonsai. Edible bonsai enthusiasts want a tree of some size that will produce a crop within a few years at most, rather than waiting decades or centuries for the tree to mature. Plants also need more food when producing a harvestable crop. Faster-growing herbs and scented geraniums in particular can be heavy feeders. I like to mix a slow time-release fertilizer with about a nine-month time span into the potting soil; fertilizer can also be used as a top dressing on an established bonsai. When a bonsai is actively growing or producing fruit I often fertilize again at least once a month while watering. A mild fertilizer like fish emulsion can even be used on a weekly or bimonthly basis to

These variegated calamondin oranges were planted together to create an orange grove reaching a height of twenty-six inches.

provide constant nutrients to actively growing or fruiting bonsai. One drawback of fish emulsion is its odor: some species are grown particularly for their fragrance, which is not improved by the smell of rotting fish. A general-purpose balanced fertilizer should be used when mixing a slow time-release plant food into the soil. Monthly or bimonthly extra fertilizer treatments can be used to provide special needs like acidity for plants that like acid soil, or to deliver a high nitrogen dose to a bonsai in an active vegetative growing phase; a fertilizer higher in phosphorus and potassium can be used to stimulate flower and fruit production. A fertilizer high in nitrogen, which pushes vegetative rather than flowering growth, is always good for herbs and scented geraniums where the harvest primarily comes

This nice harvest of strawberry guavas was combined with a similar quantity of lemon guavas and fermented into two cases of wine.

Above: A ripe kumquat seen close up.

Left: This kumquat has been in training for about five years from a five-gallon nursery stock plant. The fifty-eight-inch specimen is carrying more than fifty ripe kumquats.

from the foliage. This is especially true if one is trying to cultivate bonsai from a species that grows and flowers very rapidly, like basil.

In more than twenty years of growing commercial bonsai from faster-growing species that can grow year-round and live indoors, I have always found that my plants respond well to heavier fertilization programs. Of course, we were in production and trying to produce attractive bonsai as quickly as possible. Using fast-growing varieties allows for the creation and maintenance of bonsai over months and years instead of decades and centuries. This fits well with commercial production as well as modern society's desire for instant gratification. Creating a good-sized, attractive bonsai in a short period of time greatly expands the potential of this art form, and makes it easier for newcomers to consider training bonsai.

Another consideration is the desire to harvest a usable crop from a bonsai. This changes some of the basic concepts of bonsai cultivation from severe miniaturization of large trees to shaping small- to mid-sized trees into medium- to large-sized bonsai up to eight feet tall. To encourage production that is more than just symbolic, a good-sized bonsai is needed, and feeding provides the nutrients that will support your crop. Whether the harvest is fruit or foliage, excess growth fed by regular fertilization will be regularly removed from the bonsai.

Many of the species discussed in this book—notably guavas, citrus, and especially edible figs—have larger leaves and greater internode distance between leaves than traditional bonsai. Such plants may need regular pinching over several years to develop a classic full crown. Growing tips need to be pinched regularly, leaving no more than two or three nodes between each pinch. If the plant is grown for its foliage, this will provide a regular fresh harvest. If your bonsai is a species that flowers and fruits, you need to be aware of the flowering season and be careful not to remove flower buds or fruit when pinching the growing tips. If the harvest is important, it is sometimes best to let the bonsai grow a little unchecked, allowing it to flower and fruit before trimming it back to the desired shape.

Many of these species will sprout new shoots regularly from the trunk, main branches, exposed roots, or soil. As a rule, these should be removed as soon as they show. Sometimes a strong new shoot sprouting from a main branch can be allowed to develop into a new section of the crown. Most citrus plants sold commercially are grafted onto a rootstock that may be from another species entirely. The rootstock will send out strong shoots that look very different from the desirable top of the tree, and these should be removed immediately. A six-foot tall citrus bonsai can often sprout new shoots above the graft from the trunk and bare main branches that will flower and bear fruit when only a few inches long. Watch your citrus shoots closely and perhaps let them develop a bit to see if they start to flower. Clusters of fruit will hide the classic lines of your bonsai's trunk, but the ripe fruit will look stunning. The short twigs can be removed after flowering or fruiting.

We are changing the philosophy here from trying to create the "ideal" ornamental bonsai to a compromise between perfect form and bountiful harvests. In my opinion, the attractiveness of the flowers or fruit overshadows any short-term imperfections in form. Not everyone agrees: try displaying a large blooming rosemary or a variegated calamondin orange with flowers and ripe fruit at a Bonsai Society show. A few other exhibitors will start muttering to each other about the imperfections in your bonsai. You might even hear, "This is *not* real bonsai!" Meanwhile, the largest crowd in the show, including many of the other exhibitors, will be gathered around your specimen

This twenty-five-year-old hibiscus bonsai needs some pruning, but flowers frequently through the winter in front of an east facing sliding glass door.

Drastic pruning was needed for this large, neglected pineapple guava to be reshaped as a bonsai. A couple months after a severe pruning, it was potted into a deep bonsai pot.

This fifty-five-inch pineapple guava has been trained for twelve years. It started as a one-gallon nursery plant.

oohing and ahhing, saying, "This is the neatest bonsai I've ever seen!" Take full advantage of every feature when you display your edible bonsai. Serve a tea made from its foliage, perhaps with limequat marmalade (from another bonsai) on crackers. Plan a dinner party with a bonsai theme using foliage and/or fruit from your various bonsai in every course, from wine to dessert, with your prized bonsai as the centerpiece. Consuming part of your art while it continues to flourish, grow, and change carries it to a unique new level.

With the hectic schedule of the modern lifestyle, it can be easy to let a large, fast-growing specimen get out of hand. You will need to keep it sized to fit in the available space. If your edible bonsai grows too fast, it

This variegated Calamondin orange has been in training for two years after being cut back severely from an overgrown five-gallon nursery plant. This specimen is forty-two inches tall.

may require a severe pruning to keep the size in check. Rest assured, how-ever, that it will regrow quickly. I have trimmed citrus, figs, guavas, and a number of my other bonsai back to bare one- or two-inch diameter stubs and watched them grow a tight new crown within months.

The variegated calamondin orange pictured in Chapter 3, "Bountiful Bonsai Possibilities," was created from a five-gallon nursery plant. It sat in a neglected corner of my busy bonsai greenhouse for several years, eventu-ally developing a weak, loose, open crown that was too large for the trunk and hung near the ground. Finally it became infected with mealy bugs. After pruning the entire crown down to the trunk and a couple branch stubs with no foliage, I cleaned the specimen thoroughly and repotted it into clean soil in a nursery pot. After two years of regrowth with constant pinching, it was repotted into into a bonsai pot; six months after that it was photographed for this book.

This lemon guava has been moved from a training pot to nice pottery.

The lemon guava shown on this page was a prized plant that had been allowed to grow with little pruning for several years to maximize crop production. It grew to twelve feet tall and had rooted out the bottom of its ceramic pot, with one-inch-diameter roots disappearing into the floor of the greenhouse. After cutting the entire crown back to six feet tall, I smashed the ceramic pot with a hammer to protect the roots, which I then dug out of the ground. Less than a year after this stub of a tree was set in its bonsai pot, it bore the fruit in the picture. Those lemon guavas, mixed with some strawberry guavas, are currently aging in my wine cellar.

In the spring of 2012, during the massive wildfires that ravaged Colorado, I was evacuated for twelve days while a forest fire burned within a hundred yards of my home and greenhouse. A neighbor who didn't evacuate was kind enough to water my greenhouse, but missed a thirty-six hour period where the outside temperatures reached a hundred degrees and there was no power to run the cooling system. Some of the bonsai illustrated in this book died completely; some died to the ground and sprouted out again; and all were damaged. After being pruned back, the plants that lived are starting to look good again.

This strawberry guava was pruned down to sixty-seven inches after being dug out of the ground in the greenhouse. Four months later, it was seventy-six inches tall, as shown here.

A group of strawberry guavas that were also rooted into the ground and brushing the fourteen-foot ceiling of the greenhouse turned totally brown and died back halfway to the ground. When new shoots began sprouting from the bottom six feet, I dug these trees out and pruned them to a basic trunk and branch stubs. Some of these stubs are two inches in diameter and have dozens of new shoots sprouting below the cut. I removed the undesirable shoots and regularly pinch those that are left to fill out a new crown. Although they are between six and eight feet tall, these guavas will be spectacular bonsai with nice crowns and should bear a good crop of fruit a little more than a year after undergoing the damage and severe pruning.

When visiting people's homes, you often see the same variety of house-plants. Ficus, palms, Dracaenas, Sheffleras, jades, spider plants, and a few others are ubiquitous, with a few other species in the mix. Edible bonsai can be grown in the same spaces as these common plants. Whether you just have a little space for a tabletop bonsai or a sunroom with space for several six-foot edible bonsai, it can be very satisfying to produce an edible crop from your indoor plants. Perhaps this is the ultimate statement in going green and eating locally. Now you can have your bonsai and eat it, too.

CHAPTER 6

The Bountiful Harvest

T he main purpose of this book is to help you create bonsai that will bear a harvestable crop for home use. A small collection of bonsai can provide a surprising variety of flavors to add to your cooking. While I will include some specific recipes here, most of my personal bonsai harvest is used in two ways. I use small amounts to accent and add flavor to dishes I already make regularly. Herbs can be dried, and fruits can be frozen, lasting for a year or more to be used as needed. The various herbs and the small citrus that can be eaten peel and all, such as the calamondin orange, kumquat, and limequat, are especially useful in this way. A single fruit from these small citrus can be enough to flavor an entire dish. During the cold, snowy winters at my mountain home, my citrus bonsai carry enough ripe fruit to use in cooking every week; they are the most productive and useful specimens in my entire collection.

It is also possible to create long-lasting foods from your bonsai's production. With a larger harvest, or by combining several small harvests saved by drying or freezing, there are several ways to preserve your bonsai crop for years. Small fruits can be canned in sugar syrup, or made into jams, jellies, or chutneys. These can then be used like the fresh fruit to flavor dishes. One batch of rosemary jelly canned in small jars can provide a continuous supply of unique, sweet rosemary flavor to use in the kitchen. My favorite way to preserve a bonsai harvest is to make wine that can be savored for years, or even decades. Herbs, flowers, and fruits from bonsai specimens have contributed to my wine cellar for more than twenty years.

Perhaps the simplest bonsai are the various herbs, which are highly productive. A single rosemary, thyme, sage, or savory bonsai can provide enough fresh and dried herbs to supply a household for an entire year. Pick the leaves fresh to chop and use as needed. When shaping your bonsai, dry the leaves for later use. If you enjoy grilling, save your herb stems, soak them in water, and throw them on the coals to flavor meats, vegetables or fruits. Basil doesn't keep its flavor well when dried, but fortunately grows quickly enough to provide a nearly continuous fresh harvest. The best way to preserve an oversupply of basil is by freezing it. Put it in a blender with just enough water to whip it up into a thick green slurry, then freeze it in ice cube trays. These frozen basil cubes will keep their flavor for a year and are very useful in the kitchen: one cube will perk up any dish. Another way to preserve these culinary flavors is to make herbal jellies. Mint jellies are generally served with lamb, but rosemary jelly makes a wonderful glaze on roast turkey. Making herb jellies is as simple as brewing a strong tea and adding sugar and commercial pectin. Use a mint jelly recipe and substitute your favorite herb for the mint. Herbal jellies are delightful spread on toast or crackers, and can be added to glazes and sauces of all kinds. Tuck a fresh rosemary sprig into a jar of bonsai rosemary jelly before sealing to create a unique holiday gift.

Other fragrant plants such as lemon verbena, lavender, pineapple sage, Costa Rican mint, and scented geraniums are considered more useful as potpourri or herbal teas, but they all can be used in the kitchen to provide unique accents to dishes. Don't be afraid to experiment with your herbs in new ways that aren't covered in traditional cookbooks. Try substituting lemon thyme for regular thyme, or adding lemon verbena when

preparing eggs with fresh herbs. Both rosemary and thyme make a stimu-
lating hot tea on a cold winter morning. Soothing lavender tea can be
made with foliage trimmings as well as the flowers of French lavender.
Flowers such as hibiscus and jasmine, as well as the petals of any citrus
flower, make great additions to herbal tea blends, or can be used to flavor
green tea. Small citrus that are edible whole, like kumquat, limequat, and
calamondin orange, can be sliced thin, dried, and chopped or crumbled
to add to your tea blends. Herbs like pineapple sage, lemon verbena, and
Costa Rican mint have intense yet very pleasant fragrances that are almost
intoxicating when used as aromatherapy. One of my favorite uses for these
herbs is to garnish a mixed drink or even lemonade with a fresh sprig that
brushes the nose with every sip. Aromatherapy can be very beneficial even
if it just brightens your mood and brings a smile to your face. If you have
fragrant herbal bonsai, touch them and breathe in the fragrance every
day. Don't forget to stop and smell the flowers when your jasmine, myrtle,
Natal plum, or citrus is in bloom.

Tea is nice, but sometimes a drink with a little more kick is desired.
Dandelion wine is not the only flower wine—I have hibiscus-flower wine
and jasmine-flower wine in my cellar. I've used a quart of jasmine per gallon and a couple quarts of dried hibiscus per gallon of wine to turn out
these delicate vintages. Making flower wines essentially involves brewing
a strong tea, adding sugar and wine yeast, and then waiting as your tea
turns into wine. Adding raisins as part of the sugar gives the wine more
body and character, and is especially helpful with flower and herb wines
that don't contain any other fruit. You'll find winemaking supplies and
detailed instructions at your local home-brewing store. Basic equipment
includes a covered bucket for primary fermentation and a large glass bottle with a fermentation lock for secondary fermentation and aging.

I used four one-quart jars packed full of dried jasmine flowers, fifteen
pounds of sugar, two pounds of golden raisins, and a packet of wine yeast
to make two cases of jasmine-flower wine with the following recipe: Pour
two gallons of boiling water over the flowers and chopped raisins, then

add another gallon of water in which five pounds of sugar have been dissolved. When cool, add wine yeast. Stir twice a day. After several days, add another five pounds of sugar dissolved in water; after several more days, repeat once more. After ten to fourteen days of this primary fermentation, strain out the flowers and raisin pulp and pour the fermenting wine into a glass container, sealing it with a fermentation lock. You can use gallon jugs or five-gallon glass carboys from a home-brew store for this. Your wine will finish fermenting and start to age, and will be ready to drink or bottle in three to six months. This same recipe can be followed to make herbal wines, which are great for sipping and incredible when used in cooking.

I have been accused of being obsessed with winemaking. Admittedly, I am past the middle of a third decade of building a cellar containing several hundred cases of homemade wine. My cellar contains wines made from most of the edible bonsai discussed in this book. There are rosemary and thyme wines made from bonsai trimmings that have been aging in my cellar for more than twenty years; my oldest is a lavender wine from 1986. The artistic symmetry of drinking a decades-old wine made from a bonsai while viewing bonsai that have been in training that long is very appealing. I treasure my bonsai harvests, and the best way to preserve that harvest to enjoy for years is to make wines that can age along with the plants themselves.

Herbal and citrus wines can be intense, and are great served as an aperitif in small servings. For cooking, however, nothing else can compare. They can be used in sauces or marinades and splashed over any sauté. Use them to baste foods cooking on the grill, or as an ingredient in homemade salad dressing. My favorite way to prepare a turkey is to use one of those oven-baking bags and one to three cups of wine, depending on size, to steam it and infuse it with flavor. A chicken or any type of roast may be cooked the same way. The meat will be tender and juicy and the leftover liquid will make great gravy or soup stock.

Flower and fruit wines are more conventional and easier to drink a bottle of over dinner. As mentioned above, jasmine and hibiscus flowers

A few of my vintages: Lemon Lemon Drop, Citrus Symphony blend, and Strawberry Lemon Guava wine.

can be dried and saved for making wine. Figs, guavas, and some citrus make heartier fruit wines. Mellow citrus like orange, blood orange, and even kumquat can make delightful wines by using a couple gallons of fruit with water, sugar, and wine yeast to make five gallons of wine. Sharper-tasting citrus like lemons, limes, and limequats make more intense wines, especially if a greater quantity of fruit is used per gallon of wine. My favorite cooking wine is made from lemon basil, lime basil, lemons, and limes fermented together. It's a citrus explosion on the palate when sipped, and adds great flavor to any dish. One of my favorite tricks when cooking rice is to add half a cup of herbal wine to the rice for the last five minutes of steaming. This adds delightful flavor to steamed rice; different wines can be paired with specific main dishes to be served alongside.

I never use sulfites, which are supposed to kill yeast and "preserve" wines, yet my vintages have lasted for decades and improved with age. In fact, an opened partial bottle kept corked in the fridge can be used for months without it going bad, making it possible to have several different cooking wines open for regular use in the kitchen to provide variety. Making wine is definitely my favorite way to preserve an edible bonsai harvest. It is not too difficult, and one five-gallon fermentation bottle on your counter can make two or three batches of wine a year. Learn to do this and you will have a unique supply of wines for cooking, drinking and special gifts.

The most prized and useful part of my bonsai harvest is the citrus. This is in part because I take pleasure in being able to produce a usable citrus crop in a colder northern climate. It is more difficult to produce large citrus like oranges or grapefruits indoors, but lemons and limes are easier, and the smaller limequats, kumquats and calamondin oranges can be extremely productive and are exceptional, peel and all—with seeds removed—for use in cooking. Key limes can also be used like this if sliced very thinly. Kumquats are smaller and you may need to use several for the same amount of flavor as one of the larger citrus. These intensely flavored fruits are sour, and may need to have sugar or honey added when used in

Limequat marmalade and toast.

Ingredients for sautéed asparagus with peppers, basil, garlic, cashews, and calamondin orange.

desserts. They can be used to flavor yogurt or homemade sorbet and ice cream. Whole kumquats and quartered, seeded limequats or oranges can used as an edible garnish for mixed drinks.

The small citrus really shine in cooking, however. They can be used fresh, frozen, or canned; you can even use the pulp left over after fermenting into wine. Limequats and calamondins, which have sharply different flavors, make an intensely flavored marmalade to be spread on toast or added to any sauce that would benefit from that sweet-tart flavor. You can substitute the finely chopped, seeded fruits, plus a little added water, in any orange marmalade recipe that uses commercial pectin. Gently warm some marmalade with a splash of citrus or herbal wine, add spices if you like, and use as a final glaze on grilled meat or a roast bird. Rosemary or thyme would be good with this—or, for a unique twist, flavor the glaze with Chinese five-spice blend.

Small citrus are at their best used fresh. Any of them can be chopped and added to your favorite sauté or stir-fry. A simple favorite is to sauté asparagus with almonds and garlic in olive oil, then chop a seeded calamondin orange and add with the garlic. You'll get a nice citrus note with the asparagus and a sharp citrus burst when you bite into a piece of peel. Chopped, seeded citrus can also be added to eggs in an omelet, scramble, or soufflé. Try onion, garlic, celery, red pepper, cashews, mushrooms, and a limequat for a lively combination. The bright flavor that comes with the citrus enhances everything.

A dish I like to take to parties is a Salmon Citrus Cheese Ball. In olive oil, sauté onion, garlic, ginger, celery, bell peppers (red, yellow, and green), one hot pepper, cashews, parsley, and two chopped, seeded limequats or calamondins. Add about four ounces of flaked salmon (you can also use crab or chopped shrimp). Splash in some herb or citrus wine with the seafood and finish the sauté. Stir the resulting three to four cups of sautéed veggies and salmon into a package of cream cheese while still hot, then chill and roll into a ball. Roll the cheese ball in crushed nuts if you like. If you don't overcook the vegetables, then your cheese ball will be crunchy

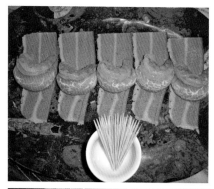

Top: These Bacon-Shrimp Citrus Wraps, made with blood orange segments, are ready to roll.

Center: Rolled and pinned appetizers ready for the grill.

Bottom: Bacon-Shrimp Citrus Wraps fresh from the grill.

and full of veggies and nuts, with just enough flavored cheese to hold it together—it's actually a healthy dish. You can easily substitute or add any other fruit, vegetables, nuts, spices, even mushrooms, to customize this recipe to your taste.

Citrus Fire Chicken is a simple main dish that is quick and easy to prepare. Cut one boneless chicken breast per serving into long thin strips. Sauté the strips in coconut oil with one or more hot peppers of your choice and one chopped, seeded limequat or calamondin for every two breasts. Add a couple of spoonfuls of citrus marmalade near the end for some sweetness to balance the fire. Serve this as your meat course, alongside rice, or on top of a salad. Peeled, chopped blood oranges or chopped kum-quats could also be used for the citrus. Hopefully your hot pepper bonsai will provide the fire.

My favorite appetizer, Bacon-Shrimp Citrus Wraps, is made with segmented blood oranges, although I've also used tangerine segments when I can't wait for my blood oranges to get ripe. Use very ripe oranges with deep color for the best effect. Take one medium to large shelled and deveined shrimp along with one blood orange segment, wrap with a half strip of turkey bacon, and pin with one or two toothpicks. (Note: I use turkey bacon, not only because it is healthier than pork, but also because it is made from pre-cooked turkey and only needs to be browned. With pork bacon, the shrimp and citrus would be overcooked, if not burned, by the time the bacon was

Grilled Bacon-Shrimp Citrus Wraps served alongside a sautéed orange asparagus dinner.

ready.) Spray or brush with olive oil and season to taste. I recommend a combination of powdered garlic, ginger, paprika, and lemon pepper. Cook on the grill, turning frequently. Depending on the heat, the appetizer will take ten to fifteen minutes to cook. You might spritz them with a little herbal or citrus wine while cooking, especially if the fire is hot. Finish with a glaze of your choice for the last two minutes, exposing the glaze to the heat briefly. I've used all kinds of prepared oriental sauces, even cocktail sauce, for the glaze. My favorite is a blend of Thai sweet chili sauce and either citrus marmalade or a fruit jam like apricot. I advise you to make twice as many of these appetizers as you think you'll need. If you serve them at a dinner party and turn your back for two minutes, they'll be gone.

Dried figs are easy to find, but fresh figs are rare unless you live in a warm climate where they survive outdoors. I've never really cooked with figs, although when I started growing fig bonsai I saved and froze every fig until I had enough to create a vintage of fig wine. I serve them fresh, halved or quartered, on salads or as an edible garnish on a serving plate. My Kadota and Peter's Honey figs are a beautiful golden yellow when cut, and my Celeste figs are a deep ruby red. Brown Turkey figs are a

This Kadota fig got so ripe it opened like a flower.

Pineapple guava flower petals are white on the outside and red on the inside but curl shortly after opening, hiding the red inside.

purple-brown color and larger than most other figs. Using figs of different colors as a garnish makes a beautiful presentation. When I serve them as an appetizer, I trim off the stem end and stuff a nugget of feta cheese inside. Small figs can be served whole after stuffing; larger ones can be halved or quartered, with a nugget of feta placed in each piece.

Strawberry and lemon guavas have tart skins and soft, sweet, white flesh when ripe. They also contain hard seeds a little larger than grape pips that are tough to remove without losing some of the tasty flesh. If the guavas are fresh, it's probably best to just eat them and spit out the seeds. Guavas make a nice jelly when cooked down if the seeds are sieved or strained out before the pectin and sugar are added. I either eat my guavas fresh or ferment them into wine. My pineapple-guava bonsai flower every year but have never produced fruit; apparently they are not self-fertilizing. Pineapple guavas need some age to flower, but are worth growing for the flowers even without fruit. The large white petals are thick, fleshy and sweet, and are best picked from the tree and eaten fresh. They can be a unique edible garnish or topping on a salad.

While I have grown every plant variety mentioned in this book, some of them have never borne an edible crop for me. That doesn't prevent them from being interesting bonsai to grow, and I still hope that perhaps with more age or experimentation they will bear fruit. Some are just small shrubs like Chilean guava, which provides a few tasty berries but not enough to make anything without saving several years' worth of fruit in the freezer. Natal plums are tasty and produce fruit sporadically through the year, but I've never had enough of them to make anything substantial. Most edible-bonsai growers will have similar results, unless they have the space for a large bonsai or a group of several smaller bonsai of the same species. Most of these fruits are best enjoyed fresh right from the tree. Some fruits, like citrus, can flavor an entire dish, but perhaps the best use of a special, unique fruit is to pluck one off the bonsai to offer fresh to a guest who has never tasted a fresh fig, guava, or kumquat.

We create bonsai in order to share their beauty with others. With edible bonsai, that includes letting others experience the consumable part of the bonsai. When someone visits my greenhouse, if there is no fresh fruit to offer, I share fragrances of flowers like citrus or Natal plum, or I pluck a leaf from a rosemary or Costa Rican mint bush to hand them for aromatherapy, or I have them simply touch my fragrant herbal bonsai with their hands and breathe in the fragrance. I have attended Bonsai Society shows where some exhibitors watch their prized specimens like hawks, and there are more signs saying "Please Don't Touch the Bonsai" than there are bonsai. I've brought large herbal bonsai, which grow so quickly that I could trim pieces of the bonsai to give away with damaging my specimen, to these shows, and encouraged people to come touch them and experience the fragrance. I'm afraid I created a fuss and attracted a crowd that interfered with foot traffic through the exhibit. You'll find that people respond to the concept of approachable bonsai gardening with great interest. I wish you well as you amaze your friends with your bountiful bonsai!

INDEX

Published by Tuttle Publishing, an imprint of Periplus Editions (HK) Ltd.

www.tuttlepublishing.com

Library of Congress Cataloging-in-Publication Data

Bender, Richard W.
  Bountiful bonsai : create instant indoor container gardens with edible fruits, herbs and flowers / Richard W. Bender.
      p. cm.
  ISBN 978-4-8053-1270-4 (pbk.)
  1. Bonsai. 2. Indoor gardening. I. Title.
  SB433.5.B43 2014
  635.9'772--dc23

2013040431

ISBN: 978-4-8053-1270-4

Distributed by:
North America, Latin America & Europe
Tuttle Publishing
364 Innovation Drive
North Clarendon, VT 05759-9436 U.S.A.
Tel: (802) 773-8930
Fax: (802) 773-6993
info@tuttlepublishing.com
www.tuttlepublishing.com

Japan
Tuttle Publishing
Yaekari Building, 3rd Floor
5-4-12 Osaki
Shinagawa-ku
Tokyo 141 0032
Tel: (81) 3 5437-0171
Fax: (81) 3 5437-0755
sales@tuttle.co.jp
www.tuttle.co.jp

Asia Pacific
Berkeley Books Pte. Ltd.
61 Tai Seng Avenue #02-12
Singapore 534167
Tel: (65) 6280-1330
Fax: (65) 6280-6290
inquiries@periplus.com.sg
www.periplus.com

First edition
18 17 16 15 14   5 4 3 2 1

Printed in Malaysia 1409TW

The Tuttle Story:
Books to Span the East and West

Many people are surprised to learn that the world's largest publisher of books on Asia had its humble beginnings in the tiny American state of Vermont. The company's founder, Charles E. Tuttle, belonged to a New England family steeped in publishing.

Immediately after WW II, Tuttle served in Tokyo under General Douglas MacArthur and was tasked with reviving the Japanese publishing industry. He later founded the Charles E. Tuttle Publishing Company, which thrives today as one of the world's leading independent publishers.

Though a westerner, Tuttle was hugely instrumental in bringing a knowledge of Japan and Asia to a world hungry for information about the East. By the time of his death in 1993, Tuttle had published over 6,000 books on Asian culture, history and art—a legacy honored by the Japanese emperor with the "Order of the Sacred Treasure," the highest tribute Japan can bestow upon a non-Japanese.

With a backlist of 1,500 titles, Tuttle Publishing is more active today than at any time in its past—inspired by Charles Tuttle's core mission to publish fine books to span the East and West and provide a greater understanding of each.